SPIRITUALLY PARENTED

Rachel, So
H's done! So
grateful for your
presence in my
life & appreciate
your support.
Excited for you
to dive in!
Meg ♡

SPIRITUALLY PARENTED

A Foot in Both Worlds

MEG GIBBS

NEW DEGREE PRESS
COPYRIGHT © 2023 MEG GIBBS
All rights reserved.

SPIRITUALLY PARENTED
A Foot in Both Worlds

ISBN   979-8-88926-715-7 *Paperback*
        979-8-88926-716-4 *Ebook*

LIBRARY OF CONGRESS CONTROL NUMBER: 2023912068

Mom, we did the thing!

And to the ancient healing magic that continues to evolve and weave together the wisdom of the past, current, and future generations—thank you for dancing with me this lifetime.

Contents

Author's Note   9

PART 1		**15**
Chapter 1.	Opening Prayer	17
Chapter 2.	Make Space for Magic	21
Chapter 3.	For the Love of Each Other	25
Chapter 4.	From the Beginning	31
Chapter 5.	Leaning In and Learning	35
Chapter 6.	Walking the Wheel	43
Chapter 7.	East Child	51
Chapter 8.	The Last Workshop	63
Chapter 9.	Searching for Acceptance	69
Chapter 10.	Spiritual Surprises	79
Chapter 11.	Guided Meditation	89
PART 2		**93**
Chapter 12.	Spiritual Teachers and Trusting Yourself	95
Chapter 13.	Anxiety and Surrender	103
Chapter 14.	Sharing Energy	113
Chapter 15.	Loving Movement	119
Chapter 16.	Everyone Has Their Own Montana	129
Chapter 17.	Concentric Circles of Connection	141
Chapter 18.	Intuitive Work	149
Chapter 19.	Finding My Place in Two Worlds	163

PART 3	169
Chapter 20. Light Lifting Ceremony	171
Chapter 21. Stripped Down	179
Chapter 22. Intuition in Action	191
Chapter 23. Create What's Missing	199
Chapter 24. Re-member Who You Are	207
Chapter 25. Follow the Childhood Threads	215
Chapter 26. Facing the Unknown	225
Chapter 27. Centering the Body	231
Chapter 28. Raise Your Energetic Awareness	237
Chapter 29. To Keep in Your Back Pocket	243
Chapter 30. Closing Prayer	249
Acknowledgments	253
Appendix	255
Author Bio	257

Author's Note

In the epigraph to Matt Burgess's book *Enormous Smallness*, e.e. cummings states, "It takes courage to grow up and become who you truly are" (Burgess 2015). I believe this is accentuated in a society that does not support the outliers, weirdos, and nonconformists. So if you identify as one of those—you are my people!

My moms raised me to believe in and connect with Spirit. For me, the name I call into the night stars has changed over time: from praying to the Goddess, asking for support from the Universe, and nestling into a deep relationship with Great Spirit. I didn't always accept or embrace this spiritual journey, and for a long time, I resisted walking a healer's path.

I'm a bit of a skeptic, which has served me well. This has led me to be discerning with what resonates and, ultimately, aligns with my soul.

I am a Certified Somatic Spiritual Coach, which means I help people connect with their body, mind, and Spirit. This work combines my extensive dance background, shamanic spiritual lineage, and leadership development courses to create intuitive, embodied healing practices. I am credentialed as a Professional Certified Coach through the International Coach Federation (ICF) and have worked with private clients one on one since 2013. I've led workshops in the movement and personal growth realm for over fifteen years and specialize in helping people bring forth their intuitive side and authentically weave more of who they are into what they do.

I define Spirituality simply as having a relationship with Spirit—to believe in something "bigger than us." Some people consider Spirit to mean god, a connection to nature, a specific religious community, or an intangible sense there's something greater out there—but aren't sure exactly what it is or what to call it.

I experience Spirit as a "felt knowing" in my body. Whether it is a tingling at the crown of my head or a punch in the gut, it feels undeniable. I started hearing little messages from my body that differed from my everyday thoughts. I started to "know" things and see things others didn't when I was really young. As a sensitive kid, I often got made fun of for my weirdness. But here's the twist—I turned my weirdness into wisdom, and now I get paid for it!

Counter to most spiritual adults I've met, I grew up in a family who embraced and nurtured the "weird" parts of me that ultimately transformed into celebrated spiritual gifts. I went through periods where my natural sacred abilities were heightened and other times when they were more closed off but never completely shut down. That is a really important distinction because many people I've worked with had their gifts completely squashed or painfully shamed out of them as children by parents who didn't understand.

As we get to know one another through this book, please "take what works and leave the rest." This is definitely not a "how-to" guide but rather my takeaways from growing up in a household that valued an engaged spiritual practice. I invite you to feel your way through these stories and see how the lessons and exercises land in your body. While this may be an unusual ask, it's a powerful tool for discernment and learning to trust your gut.

Mom and I shared the dream of writing a book together. Professionally, my mom was a therapist, Reiki master, and Shamanic Spiritual Teacher. She was also my best friend, was a supreme advice giver, and brought a powerful sacred presence into my life. She introduced me to Spirit and gave me amazing teachers, guides, and family along the way. Unfortunately, she died of cancer in 2012.

We didn't get the chance to coauthor a book while she was alive, but luckily, we continue to have a powerful connection even though she's crossed to the other side. The words I've written are a combination of my own and a blend of "spiritual consultations" I have with my guides, allies, ancestors, and spiritual team.

Mom is still very present in this process, and I look forward to sharing our stories, teachings, and lessons to support you on your path forward.

This book offers opportunities for self-reflection: first, an invitation to deepen your own connection with Spirit and second, to re-parent and give yourself the support you may have needed but didn't receive as a kid. Or if you are a parent, to learn ways to nurture your own child's spiritual gifts.

Don't worry, I'm not here to convert you to any specific belief system. I may challenge some ways of thinking to take you deeper into what's true—for *you*. That's the most important approach: to come back to what resonates in *your* heart, *your* mind, and *your* body. Trust that above anything anyone else says.

I'm writing from the perspective of growing up in a spiritual family. I'm not a parent and am not giving "parenting advice." I'm sharing what went well, the drawbacks, and being raised in a more intuitive way. This has led to continually wanting to honor both the human and divine realms within us all.

To the parents who picked up this book to learn more about supporting your child, just know you're invited into your own self-discovery journey first, to tap into what is authentic and right for you. Because, ultimately, we cannot lead someone else until we have discovered our own path.

If some of these concepts are new to you, you are invited to make space to play with and enjoy the process, especially if it feels uncomfortable or outside the norm. I have a deep passion for making personal growth enjoyable because without a bit of lightness and humor, why even bother?

I really value range, including a wide array of feelings, experiences, and tones, sometimes describing death with humor or the most sacred ceremony with a pop culture reference. Because we, as humans, encompass so much.

We are both human and divine simultaneously and have access to both sides. Throughout this book, the theme of feeling forced to choose one or the other is ultimately set aside to live a more integrated life where your humanness and sacred self are both fully acknowledged.

I actually want to slow things down and take a breath together.

If you're up for it, pause and check in with your body.

What do you notice?

Have you ever done this before?

Are you experiencing tension? Curiosity? Excitement?

All answers are correct. This is about your experience, which is totally valid. No right or wrong answers.

For instance, in my body, I feel a sense of letting go and settling into my seat. If I can't get it right or wrong, it gives me permission to just *be*, to feel at peace. My shoulders drop a bit, and my breath starts to expand and take up more space in my rib cage.

I trust what brought you here and the divine timing that connects us through these pages at this exact moment.

I rely deeply on intuition and will invite you to lean into and explore your own inner guidance. There is no cookie-cutter method to finding what works for you. It's about resonance, alignment, and trusting yourself. So if you're used to "going by the book," this may be a new approach. I'll ask questions along the way to invite you to slow down and check in with yourself.

You may even want to keep a journal or notes in the margins. This book is meant to be "lived in." It doesn't have to stay pristine. Wrestle with the concepts, discuss with friends, disagree with me, discover something new, and ultimately come back to what feels good in your body.

One of my pet peeves is that nearly every spiritual workshop I've attended only involves sitting and taking in information intellectually. Not this time! Let's engage on a soul, heart, mind, and body level as we move through this together.

I welcome you to this book.

Will you take one more deep breath for now?

Fully in and fully out.

This book is for people who want to take the next steps on their spiritual path and are ready to journey home to themselves.

To know you're okay.

To cherish not being "normal" and embrace your own intuitive gifts.

To uncover—or maybe rediscover—what truth feels like in your body.

I am excited for you to feel into the idea that you are loved solely because you are alive and breathing. Simply for existing, you are loved.

Thank you for letting me walk beside you.

May our blessings be abundant and the lessons be gentle along the way.

With deep love,
Meg

A quick note: Some people hear the word "shaman" and think of plant medicine. While that is part of some shamanic practices, it is not part of the two main spiritual lineages I've studied most. So whenever I mention being altered, it's referring to organic energetic shifts and not in reference to working with hallucinogenic plant medicines (except for that one story you'll get to later).

PART 1

1

Opening Prayer

Aho Great Spirit,

I call you into these pages to bring these words to life with breath, energy, and support for this journey. Please surround this reader with luminescence, to allow them to take time to absorb these words.

I am so grateful for my life this day and for the opportunity to join together in this way.

Pachamama, Mother Earth, thank you for holding us and teaching us to be resilient, generative, and compassionate living in community with all living beings.

Calling in the realm of all possibilities, Father Sky, I pray to open my heart to see beyond self-imposed limitations and take courageous action.

Grandmother Moon, thank you for shining your light in the darkness, guiding us in our dreams.

Grandfather Sun, thank you for providing heat to our planet and a reflection of our inner fire.

Great Star Nation, "Campfires of the Ancestors," thank you for being an infinite space to gather and reconnect with our loved ones who have crossed over.

Plant people, thank you for teaching us about growth, sustaining life in challenging circumstances, and showing us how to participate in nature's cycle from seed to bloom and back to seed again.

Animal people, thank you for the medicine you carry and teaching us to respect the four-leggeds, winged ones, creepy crawlies, finned and furry creatures all over this planet.

Stone elders, thank you for being the record keepers and showing us the power of memories in every layer of your being.

Standing people (trees), thank you for sharing your wisdom of rootedness and interconnection to all of the elements: Earth, Air, Water, and Fire.

Sacred beings who love us, from the seen and unseen world, thank you for guiding us as we move through life.

Power animals, allies, guides, and teachers, I ask you to join us in this space to protect and love us as we walk this Earth day by day.

May we be open to a path of healing, balance, and harmony, showing up as our most authentic selves, growing and evolving with compassion and kindness.

May we practice coming back to center and hearing our higher wisdom. Listening deeply to the intuitive knowing within and around us always. Tapping into our resourcefulness as nature teaches us to give from the overflow rather than from a deficit.

May we each feel supported, held, and guided back to our heart's knowing and truth.

May we see the light and life within each other and all living things, giving gratitude for this present moment.

Before closing, I invite you, dear one, to place your hand on your heart or to step outside and take some time to place your hands on the Earth wherever you live. Send love out through your hand—like a beam of light reaching down through your body and into the core.

Breathe here and let the tears flow or the smile come. Whatever is happening for you is correct.

Envision a collective light forming by combining your light with everyone else's who is reading this right now and imagine a new expanded beam of light reaching back up through the layers of the Earth—through the floor, or whatever surface you're sitting on, and landing right back in your heart.

May this collective love shine through our bodies and amplify the connection to something bigger than us.

Please take a moment to focus on that reciprocal flow in and out of your lungs, your heart, and your hands. Ground the love in your palms as a new space to tap into and guide you.

Spirit:
When we are doubting, may we feel loved. When we are lost, may we remember the compass that lives within. When we are walking our Earth path, may we move with grace and compassion for ourselves and one another, aligning to heal and contribute to leaving the planet better than when we arrived.

May it be so.

2
Make Space for Magic

As a kid, I followed closely in Mom's footsteps of believing in a world filled with magic and mystery. When I learned Santa wasn't real, at least in the form of a literal fat white jolly man who climbed down the chimney and delivered presents all over the world in one night, I was crushed. He symbolized joy and the existence of magic and mystery embodied.

I started to question everything. "Well, if Santa isn't real then there must not be real magic at all," I said to Mom.

She looked me up and down and said with a mischievous smile, "What a sad world that would be. Just because Santa isn't actually delivering presents all over the world in one night doesn't mean magic isn't real."

Mom raised me from a young age to look beyond the physical realm and dive deep into the magic and mystery of the universe. You can imagine, as a soon-to-be middle schooler, this made me quite weird. My friends were not visiting shamans on the weekends and learning how to talk to trees.

Roald Dahl's words, "And above all, watch with glittering eyes the whole world around you because the greatest secrets are always hidden in the most unlikely places. Those who don't believe in magic will never find it (Dahl 2017)." Those words echoed in our house, and I wanted so badly to believe in the magic Mom saw in the world, but honestly, I wanted proof.

After watching the movie *Matilda* as a kid, I desperately wanted to move things with my mind. So much so that I talked with our shamanic teacher about it. She told me I would have to dedicate my life to it.

"Much like levitating. People can do it, but you have to focus solely on that one task the rest of your life," the Teacher said.

Although telekinesis fascinates me, at twelve, I didn't have the interest to deeply commit to developing one skill for my entire life.

Most of my life, I've been a "reluctant healer" and have struggled for years to fully embrace my spiritual gifts. I feared separation and rejection from my friends. It felt like the closer I got to Spirit, the farther I felt from people my own age.

What I wanted *most* in the world was to be "normal."

My godfather founded the First Existential Congregation of Atlanta, where I first explored what spirituality, beliefs, faith, and the possible existence of a higher power meant to me. One of the foundational principles the congregants learned was that you could believe in anything or nothing at all. As a kid, going to "church" meant singing "This Little Light of Mine" and playing at the park across the street. I thought everyone experienced church that way but found out many years later most kids had a *very* different reality.

"The First E," as we call it, is a congregation that holds space for a lot of questions, exploration, and community building from the ground up. When I was young, Mom was into paganism, goddess worshiping, and Earth-centric beliefs that honored the Divine Feminine. She came from a very rigid white Southern Baptist upbringing, and as an adult, she sought to undo many of the patriarchal beliefs that ruled her childhood. She grew up during a time when women didn't move out of the house unless they got married to a man, which she did shortly after graduating high school. They ultimately divorced, and Mom embarked on a long road of personal healing.

My spiritual journey is in direct correlation with Mom's. Throughout my early childhood, we believed in the Goddess, a female form of god. Women were honored, worshiped, and centered in a radical way in our home. As I grew older, Mom found shamanism and wanted to deepen her spiritual exploration of one specific sacred lineage. My own journey of discernment began when I joined her after a couple years to study shamanism with our Lakota Teacher.

Mom taught me to value magic in all its forms—scientific, spiritual, and otherwise. As I began questioning things, she told me, "You have to actively *choose* a life with magic or you'll miss out."

3

For the Love of Each Other

"You know what it's like to be loved. It's refreshing to see," said one of my mentors who stayed with me one night on a trip through Atlanta.

"What do you mean?" I asked.

"You walk through the world like a person who has been well loved." I immediately began tearing up and felt incredibly vulnerable. Her gaze steadily held mine as I tried to look away. I felt truly seen—like she discovered a secret I'd been hiding for years.

My family loved me deeply. Mom not only gave me a place in this world but she also continued carving out spaces for me *and* my weirdness to belong as I got older. She surrounded me with people I built lasting relationships with, who loved me for me and helped raise me. I was told they were part of my family, so I never questioned how we were connected.

In my early twenties, I met a friend for coffee in East Atlanta, and we stumbled onto the topic of potentially having children. We both grew up with single parents. He said, "I definitely won't have kids unless I have a partner. My mom was a single parent, and it was very hard. Not just financially, but she worked full time and raised me on her own."

"Yeah, I hear you." I paused. I knew I didn't feel that way; hard isn't the word I'd use in my family's case.

I often felt an abundance of time, chosen family, and love, even though I am a child of "divorce" (gay marriage was not legal when my moms were together and had me). They split when I was three and a half years old and lived separately from then on. I feel very lucky to have lesbian moms. I actually have three moms—two moms and a stepmom—by heterosexual standards, since if someone gets divorced and remarried, their new partner would be a stepparent.

Mom passed in 2012, before gay marriage was legal, so none of my moms were ever able to marry. As a kid, this was very scary. I remember Mom warning me that if we had to go to the hospital, there was a chance her partner of fifteen years wouldn't be allowed in the room because they were not "related."

To keep it clear:
- Mom = My biological mother, Red Earth, the parent who birthed, raised me, and passed away in 2012.
- Momma V = My second parent, Mom's partner when I was born. They separated when I was three and a half. I refer to her as my "other, other mother."
- Dreaming Bear = My stepmom, who came into our lives when I was five and helped raise me. Dreaming Bear lives in the mountains of North Georgia.
- Biological father = The sperm donor and not my "dad," since there has never been a dad in the picture.

A couple years after Mom passed, a lesbian couple friend of ours who had been together for thirty-plus years got legally married, and the second mom finally got to adopt the daughter she'd raised her entire life but had no legal tie to. Dreaming Bear and I had a similar situation. She'd been in my life for over twenty years, but on paper, she was nothing more than "my mom's friend." So we looked into adult adoption and, in 2014, made our bond legal. This important milestone solidified both our relationship and protected our family in a way we couldn't do when Mom was alive.

My moms made the courageous choice to have me through artificial insemination in the 1980s. A big part of feeling so loved was the fact I was so *wanted*. My moms were incredibly intentional, as there is no such thing as being born "a mistake" to lesbian moms. And honestly, even deeper than that, my mom really wanted to be a mom. I think mothering brought her to life.

Mom loved the earth, planting flowers, and playing in her garden. She took care of many animals, plants, and children—both her own and other people's. And she cared for herself well. Sometimes it felt like she invented self-care and setting boundaries. She took the job of mothering very seriously and knew she had to care for herself in order to care for others.

Mothering called to her, and she lit up when she put her love into action this way.

Of course, there are many kinds of mothers, but for her, it included kindness, nurturing, and a pretty high expectation of doing your best.

Mothering wasn't her sole purpose by any means, but it was certainly part of her soul's purpose.

Not in a restrictive way where women were told they needed to be a mom to be fulfilled but rather she stepped fully into her power and sacred "mother energy" when she had me. Mom *loved* being a mother. So much so that I joked if you came within a three-foot radius, she would "mother you." Our next-door neighbors had a kid, and Mom became

"Aunt B." The child I babysat in high school also called her "Aunt B." And if any of my friends came on family vacation, they were now and forever welcomed into the family.

Mom also became many of her clients' "second mother" who helped them repair relationships, heal, and re-parent their own inner child with kindness and support. Mom's philosophy was "If there's a hole, fill it." I could see as I grew older how she grew as a parent and how she re-parented herself in a nourishing and powerful way. All this active and intentional mothering happened in direct response to counteracting the way she was raised.

Mom's Spirit Name is Red Earth. In the work we did with the Lakota Teacher, after several years of study and advancement, you received your Spirit Name. It came from a journey to the spirit realm to find the two energies that came together this lifetime to form your soul's energy and sacred medicine. Receiving your Spirit Name is an honor that coincides with a rite of passage. No matter how old you are, it marks a spiritual coming of age.

In the Medicine Circles, some people go by their Spirit Name all the time while others only share it in sacred contexts. There's no prescriptive way to use your Spirit Name; it's more about carrying the energy with you—spoken or unspoken.

Mom went by Red Earth in every context. She had it written on bank checks, she shared it when she met someone new, and all the nurses and doctors who treated her through chemo knew her by that name. After my coming-of-age ceremony at fifteen, I was really proud of receiving my name and wanted to go by it all the time. However, many of my peers did not receive it well. That's a nice way of saying I got made fun of a lot and essentially decided to only share my

Spirit Name in ceremonial contexts because of the disrespect I endured.

However, both my moms are open about their Spirit Names and would introduce themselves to strangers that way, so that's how they'll be referred to. A Spirit Name is a powerful expression of the energy one carries this lifetime. So when people were mean to me, it cut deep. It's like sharing the most vulnerable part of yourself when you first meet someone but having no shield to protect you from any backlash.

When I went to college, I started going by Meg. It was neutral, short, and didn't hold any emotional charge. The challenge then arose when using my moms' names in conversation or deciding how I wanted to talk about my family. Essentially, every conversation was layered with multiple coming out moments, such as:

"Hi, I'm Meg. I have lesbian moms, who both use their Spirit Names. I started studying shamanism when I was eleven with a Lakota Teacher and do want to mention we're all white women, not indigenous. I have a deep commitment to this spiritual lineage because it speaks to my heart, and I have a large gay chosen family."

Then I'd take a breath and wait for the questions to roll in.

Honestly, this is more or less what I shared with people both as a kid *and* as a college student making new friends. I joke there's always a lot to cover up front because I can't talk about my family without mentioning their Spirit Names. And I can't share their names without giving context. After all the bases are covered, we can move forward.

The Medicine Wheel, my family, and connecting with Spirit and movement are all integrated into the lens through which I see the world. My moms and I used to attend four workshops a year—one for each season—with a Lakota Teacher. After many years of study, my mom became a Spiritual Teacher herself. Different tribes use different Wheels, some have crossover and commonalities, but I'll be speaking about what I learned from a first-person account. There was no "textbook," and everything was taught in person at experiential workshops.

This is a lifelong path of learning, which is why, when I began Life Coach training, I was appalled at some of the recommended marketing tactics. The one most commonly advised is to call yourself an "expert" after a year of studying. That feels disingenuous and ridiculous. People study a spiritual path for twenty years or more and never become a teacher or an "expert." The commodification of knowledge seems to be the focus instead of the true integration of wisdom.

I will continue to be a student on this path for the rest of my life.

4

From the Beginning

"Your soul was waiting on the edge of a star to be born," Mom told me every year around my birthday.

Our story always had a high level of magic woven into it. As she held me, she would say, "I felt when your spirit came into my womb." Mom would place her hands on her pregnant belly and send Reiki energy, saying I would swim up to her hands and nuzzle close. As a sensitive adult, I joke my connection to energy started here, even before birth.

Mom was all of the clichés—my best friend, confidant, stellar advice giver, and literally became my Spiritual Teacher when I was a teenager. Even after her death, we continue to be extremely close and talk often.

Our entire relationship is based on Mom *not* repeating her experience with her parents. They were not super close by the time I was born, and when she decided to have me, she created a powerful and abundant chosen family to help raise me. It was still not very common in the '80s for LGBTQ+ couples to have children. Some of her closest gay friends still weren't totally on board with a lesbian couple bringing a kid into the world.

But Mom was sure and brought me into this world with an enormous amount of love. In our spiritual tradition, we believe in a form of reincarnation based on the idea that your soul came here to learn certain lessons this lifetime, and once you "complete" them, you get to move on. I believe we are here to learn lessons about love, trust, safety, and boundaries. Mom and I have spent lifetimes together in various relationship structures and have a strong bond.

Water reminds me of her. She especially loved the beach. That was her special place. But when she couldn't get to the ocean, she believed deeply in the power of baths.

She would close the door, put on meditation music, place a washcloth over her eyes, and miraculously rise from the steam an hour later. Bath time was sacred. One year, I bought her a book called *Spiritual Bathing* for Christmas. Baths weren't only for decompression; it was also where she would go to tap into Spirit. Sometimes she took crystals or stones into the water to charge and meditate with. This is one of the many small, strange moments I came to accept as normal in our house.

In general, Mom was a pretty private person. As a therapist, I think she held a lot, so when she finished her day, she wanted to reset and release. She was my favorite person on the planet to make laugh. Whether playing around or watching *SNL,* she didn't hold back. Her laugh was authentic, and it became my favorite sound in the world.

I don't want to paint my childhood as overly idyllic. Of course, with all the gifts came many lessons. At home, I was embraced and nurtured, while at school and in the rest of the world, I was often criticized and felt misunderstood. I didn't fit in regardless of how much I tried. But kids my age were not talking about stone elders and Medicine Wheels at recess. They were planning to go to the mall or talking about the video games they played.

I had a tough time making friends, but eventually, I made a few very close friends who became like family and still are.

I often felt separate from kids my age—and lonely. I kept my spiritual side more private as I got older, partly as instructed by our Teacher to not share what happened at workshops and ceremonies.

In the Medicine Circles, I was a good twenty years younger than the other women, so that space also felt a bit isolating. Our Lakota Teacher set very clear confidentiality and privacy boundaries around our spiritual practices, which bonded the group together.

Some of the older students in the group told me, "It's so cool you're doing this so young and taking care of this lesson now, instead of waiting until you're fifty." The best way I can describe it, though, is I didn't really have a choice. My spiritual path never felt like a choice. It felt like a *given*... going back to conception and being born into this particular family.

I know my upbringing was "alternative," as people like to say, but the power of growing up this way showed me what it's like to be a loving parent, to value authenticity and intuition, and to walk your own path in a world that doesn't always get it.

> *One of the biggest lessons I've learned from living a Spirit-led life is our divinity and our humanity actually benefit from being present at the same time.*

They don't have to be kept separate. I think that's one of the beautiful things about growing up in an Earth-based spiritual practice; sacredness is all around us. It doesn't just exist in a church building or at a certain time. Instead, Spirit is accessible in the air we breathe and the wisdom we can tap into when we're taught to slow down and listen.

The teachings and stories from growing up this way feel important to share. Not only because they were kept private for so long but because it's never too late to re-parent yourself and actively shift your path. Much of my adulthood has focused on undoing the split I felt as a kid. I had to find my way to living a fully integrated spiritual life, while simultaneously walking with a foot in both worlds instead of choosing one over the other.

Mom did a lot to carve a path for me in the world. I didn't inherit her trauma in the same way many generations before us have. She was a cycle breaker and intentionally interrupted generational patterns to focus on healing.

In a therapy session years ago, I had an image in a meditation that Mom raked a path in the forest as I walked behind her, stopping at the fire circle, where our two energies meet. She's Earth, and I'm Fire. She created a container for me to thrive in, so my fire had a place, a safe space to exist where I was held and allowed to do my thing. When she died, it was my turn to pick up the rake and clear the rest of the path on the other side of the fire pit. This was an excruciating process to live through.

But it mirrored the idea of picking up where she left off and creating new spaces for people to step into with Spirit, as she did for me.

5

Leaning In and Learning

In college, I sat with a friend going through some difficulties in her romantic relationship, and I intuitively gave her some direction. "Start moving your hips." Then she began to sway in circles, and tears came to her eyes. As she moved the pain and energy through her body, the stuckness loosened.

I don't know how I knew to do this, but I went with it.

This is a great example of the foundation of somatic connection—linking the mind, body, and spirit and looking at the interplay between the three.

"*Somatics* describes any practice that uses the mind-body connection to help you survey your internal self and listen to signals your body sends about areas of pain, discomfort, or imbalance. These practices allow you to access more information about the ways you hold on to your experiences in your body" (Raypole 2020).

I placed my hands on my friend's heart, we took deep breaths together, and I stayed with her as she swayed. She started to slow down her hip circles, and I felt the energy dissipate. She opened her eyes pretty starkly and said, "You are such a healer." I was a bit taken aback because I definitely felt like "a student of healing." I didn't claim any professional title at that point, and it would actually take several more years before I fully stepped into that identity as a career.

I mumbled something like "thank you," but then it started to happen more and more. People would randomly share their stories with me, which often led to tears and cleansing. People have cried with me for years, and I'm a big crier, too, so I'm very comfortable with big emotions. One of the most humbling and honest aspects of this path is that healing doesn't always feel good. I don't do spiritual work because it's always a "good time" but rather because it's a *true* time. It gets to the heart of what's going on and helps you make a shift.

The moment I embraced being a healer was during a workshop in North Carolina with Don Mariano Quispe Flores. He is a highly regarded Peruvian shaman my moms and I have worked with for several years. This was my first workshop alone after Mom died. Don Mariano holds a vision of sharing the rites and teachings from the Q'ero Nation of the Andes all over the world.

The focus of the workshop was on the Pleiades—the Seven Sisters constellation—and we received initiations or "rites" to connect each star to a specific point on the body. This is one of my all-time favorite topics because it involves two pieces I care about deeply: the stars and creating an embodied practice.

Each day, we would "receive the rites," which is a new concept to most, so I'll do my best to give a concrete example. For one of the initiations, we stood in front of Don Mariano as he knelt at our feet. He took one of his stones that held sacred energy from the Pleiades and one of our stones infused with the star's energy. He then wound it around our feet in a figure eight, releasing the past and any old, heavy energy that blocked our path. He unwound and freed us for the future we were to step into.

Serene and powerful, his work is rooted in the Divine Feminine and always feels respectful and gentle. After the second day of the workshop, Don Mariano offered each of us a fifteen-minute mini-reading, where he gave us information about which star in the Pleiades we came from or had a deep connection to. Don Mariano only speaks Quechua, but his translator, who spoke many languages, offered to do my reading in Spanish instead of English. I studied Spanish in college but was nervous because I was still learning. His translator and I had been practicing together since he missed speaking Spanish away from home.

In that short conversation, I heard the phrase that changed my life: *"Eres una curandera." You are a healer.*

"Do you know that?" his translator asked me.

I knew the word *curandera* and revered it but had never used it for myself. I literally felt energy trickle down my body and immediately had a sense of recognition. The many times I'd heard the word "healer" in English had never hit me like the one time I heard that word bestowed upon me by my teacher.

At that moment, I truly "got it" for the first time. From then on, I felt comfortable saying, "I am a healer. Yo soy una curandera."

"That is what you're meant to be doing," Don Mariano went on. So, with some hesitation, at his encouragement, I started integrating more ceremonial practices into my work with coaching clients.

• • • • •

To me, my soul and body look very different, almost incongruent. Maybe that's a universal feeling when your outsides don't seem to match your insides. I cannot speak from this experience personally, but this is what I imagine it also feels like for bicultural and multilingual folks, where someone moves between both languages or cultures but may not feel like they fully belong to either.

I often felt like I had to speak one language at home and one at school or work. It's a type of spiritual code switching. However, as a kid, I didn't know that's what you're supposed to do. It took me a long time to learn this through tough consequences, unfortunately. No barrier between the sacred and my everyday experience existed as a child. I think it had a lot to do with how I was raised.

At the age of five, my moms, Red Earth and Dreaming Bear, met but chose to live apart. Because, as Mom put it, "I'm not raising my child out in the country." It's a very "red" place—and for those who don't know, Atlanta and the rest of Georgia are culturally two very different experiences.

Counter to that, "I'm not moving to the city and leaving this land for anything!" Dreaming Bear made that clear very early on in their relationship.

The diversity, community, and acceptance in the city has generally not bled into the rural areas. And my stepmom is an extremely liberal, radical out woman who has lived down a dirt road for over forty years in this small mountain town.

Mom raised me in a neighborhood in Atlanta near Little Five Points. Down the street from our old house is a park and a small strip of shops. We lived near the original Flying Biscuit Café and only a few minutes from my elementary school. Mom worked from home with clients, wore flowing skirts, and enjoyed eating at local restaurants throughout the week.

Dreaming Bear lives alone to this day and talks to all the animals around her, from the ants to the birds, snakes, and various creatures that come and go. She has a deep love of her garden and talks to the vegetables as well. Imagine Snow White, but instead of a young woman twirling in a pretty dress in the forest, there's a mountain woman who chops her own firewood with a chainsaw and is a steward of the land rather than the "owner" of it.

The question of either mom relocating never really came up. Both held strong in their values and committed to this long-distance relationship for twenty years. We had a country mouse/city mouse situation driving back and forth, so I grew up in both places.

When in North Georgia, I often felt wrapped up in the Earth and learned to value nature's pace, especially as I got older. As a young child, I had to get creative with how I spent my time because Dreaming Bear did not have a TV or WiFi. She used to read a lot of magazines for entertainment. Today, this feels unimaginable—no cartoons or distraction—and it blows my mind with how tied to technology we are nowadays.

There is still no cell service there, and I love it. I find it freeing now, but as a kid, it felt isolating, and I was sure it contributed to my internal distress of "being different." No one at school understood what it meant to spend time on the land or slow down and connect with the Earth. For both my moms, this time to unplug was important. We spent a lot of time together as a family, but sometimes Mom would send me out to play in the woods to essentially leave her in peace.

When we gathered in the evenings, we would listen to the radio and play board games. Often, on Saturday nights, we played Rummikub in the living room, while listening to *A Prairie Home Companion* with Garrison Keillor. I treasure those memories.

I read a lot when we were up in the mountains. I sat on the front porch in a comfy chair reading until my butt went numb. I relished the accomplishment of finishing a book in two days. It solidified the power of reading and moving between different worlds with an author.

As I got older, my relationship with the woods changed. I no longer thought of it as just a pretty place to go play. It also became a source of wisdom. The woods held the mysteries of the Universe, the energy of creation. A sacred connection to Mother Earth and Father Sky. I could be alone there and scream or sing without losing any privacy. I started exploring how to ask questions in nature and received responses in the form of dreams, visions, and whispers from the Universe.

I learned an important sacred lesson the hard way when I walked to the edge of a clearing one night and asked an open question. Walking into the dark pushed my comfort zone. I put my hands out in front of me and was alone with the night. The farther from the house, the darker it got and the easier it was to see the stars. They were so bright and beautiful, as though looking over us and casting their stories into the night sky.

I always felt connected with the stars and appreciated their light in the darkness. Our Lakota teacher taught us to refer to them as the "campfires of the ancestors." I love the image of people who have passed over, or souls yet to come back, hanging out around a fire together, watching over us from another plane.

I used to be very scared of the dark as a kid, and darkness in the mountains was a totally different experience than in the city. Living at the end of a dirt road with no one around for miles meant there were nights when the moon didn't brighten the sky and I couldn't see my hand in front of my face.

One time, I wanted to push my comfort zone a bit and left the house around ten p.m. I walked down the hill past where the house lights reached and felt the chill of the evening air in the darkness. I asked Spirit, "Will you teach me something, or show me something?" And very quickly, I perceived an energy body in front of me. It was about seven feet tall, off to my left. I could see it float and move just above the ground. I took a shallow breath. "What's your name?"

"Geneen," it said. I got chills because I couldn't tell what it was, and Mom didn't do this kind of thing, or at least she didn't tell me about it.

I asked a couple more questions, watching it closely. It felt like female energy with an amorphous shape. I didn't know what it was here to teach me or where exactly it came from. I could just sense it was from another realm several layers away. It wasn't an embodiment of someone who crossed over—I knew what that felt like and could distinguish it. It also felt foreign in that it did not naturally live or generate from this land. It showed itself to me because I asked it to. This still feels slightly uneasy in my body.

When I told this story to my Lakota teacher, she verbally gave me a slap on the wrist. "Don't ever go asking such an open question like that again. Anything could have happened or come to you. You need to be very deliberate with your intentions and use words that will only call in what you want to connect to." I got a little scared, like I had messed up. I was always a "good student" and didn't want to disappoint.

The Teacher checked my energy and cleared any attachments that didn't belong to me, using sage and a feather. This was the first time I had been reprimanded and felt guilty. But sometimes trial by fire, while uncomfortable, gets the point across extremely clearly. I never did it again.

Since then, I approach Spirit with specific intention and a desire to establish a loving connection, to focus on what I'm calling in and create a field of protection before reaching out to connect with the energetic realm.

That specific energy didn't feel light and good, but it wasn't overtly negative either. It just felt *off*. I learned so much from this experience. I now consciously use the words "the beings who love us" when inviting energy into sacred circles.

I set up luminescent protection around myself before adventuring into the spirit realm. And I release all the energy back from where it originated at the end.

Sometimes we learn what to do by learning what *not* to do. Luckily, there weren't huge repercussions in this instance, but it certainly impacted how I prayed and connected from then on.

I share this to support other spiritually curious folks who want to dive into energy work and are looking for guidance. Choose your words consciously and invite in "the beings who love you."

6
Walking the Wheel

The Medicine Wheel teachings have influenced and guided my life for the last twenty-five years. My deep love and appreciation for this work goes beyond words. I feel extremely privileged to have learned directly from Native American and indigenous teachers. From eleven to seventeen years old, I worked with a Lakota shaman out of Nashville.

My whole family studied with this Teacher, and my moms joined the Medicine Circles. We learned about the Lakota Medicine Wheel through four experiential workshops a year, aligning with the seasons. Everything I share I learned firsthand, not from a book or reference text. Each workshop included a theme, experiential exercises, drumming, singing, and shamanic journey work.

The Teacher designed each lesson for the group based on the information she channeled from Spirit. Shamans venture into the spirit realm to ask for divine guidance to bring back to Earth to help humanity heal and restore balance. The Medicine Wheel is the structure or vessel we use to connect all parts of ourselves: our physical body, mind, emotion, and energy.

The Medicine Wheel directions can vary by tribe. Sometimes the Wheel is made up of the four cardinal directions—North, South, East, and West—while other Wheels include

"Above, Below, and Center." Different tribes and cultures place the elements in different directions; for instance, in one Wheel, water may live in the South, while in another, the South is the place of the mountains or Earth element.

Many books have been written about the Medicine Wheel. If this calls to you, please look for Native authors and teachers who go more in depth who want to share their teachings.

I have studied with many shamans and healers from the US and South America as my spiritual practice has grown over the years. The two sacred lineages I hold are the Lakota Medicine Wheel and the rites from Don Mariano of the Andean tradition. I've received initiations from both Teachers and envision holding a river of stars in each hand that merge together at my heart, spilling through my body and down through the soles of my feet into the Earth.

Acknowledging where these teachings come from and how grateful I am to have access to this ancient wisdom is extremely important to me. There is a line between cultural appreciation and appropriation, especially for white-bodied people practicing shamanic wisdom traditions. I've seen far too many spiritual people co-opt Native American teachings, repackage them without context, and sell it as their own idea with no reference or acknowledgment of the original source.

Over the years, I have struggled with my place in learning and sharing wisdom from my spiritual path. Our Lakota Teacher taught us to keep ceremonial practices extremely private, as each new teaching had to be earned. Don Mariano, on the other hand, wants to widely share and spread the teachings all over the world to those who feel called.

I see the high level of confidentiality required as a part of being in a modern day Mystery School. Teachers passed the lessons down to their students orally, connecting past generations to a lineage of healers. Each ceremony, practice, and initiation helped raise our level of conscious awareness.

Before I go into the structure and teachings of the Medicine Wheel, I want to share how it applies to daily life. One of the main myths I want to address is that sacred work has to be separate from our normal day-to-day experience.

You are a sacred being at all times.

There is no way to "earn" or lose your inherent worthiness.

Whether you're on the floor crying, losing your temper, leaving a therapy session, or eating a bunch of chocolate—the entire time, every breath you take… you are sacred.

The phrase I keep repeating is: "Because you're breathing, you are enough. And you are enough because you are breathing."

It calms me. How does it feel for you?

Let's pause here for a breath and check in.

I see the Medicine Wheel not only as a tool but also as a lens through which to break down and process the world around us. I learned about it as a portal or a vessel for transformation. I'm going to share the structure as I learned it, before the internet, through years of study with my Teacher.

Using the mountains as a retreat space to resettle and reconnect, we would venture up to Dreaming Bear's property, surrounded by national forest on three sides where there is still no cell reception. It always felt like a true retreat tucked away in the wilderness.

Her land is a very special place to me. Years of sacred work laid the foundation. From the Lakota Teacher leading sweat lodges and vision quests, to family fire ceremonies and community herbalism workshops, I will always return to this place. Mom's energy runs through it, almost like a scent laid over the earth. Sometimes her energy is so palpable I need a break. I am extremely intentional about coming up to Bear Walks, as it's called.

The land is lush with moss-covered rocks and tree roots sticking up through the Earth. The plants grow in every direction, and it's an outrageous gift to access unmanicured land with fresh air, clean water, and wild energy.

The woods scared me a little as a kid, and it took me a long time to learn to be still and appreciate it. I've never been one to do much meditation. I prefer dancing and creating to sitting and breathing. But the balance of both has taught me to play to my strengths *and* connect in ways that stretch me.

The Medicine Wheel encompasses all of that: our strengths, woundings, challenges, and ultimately our healing.

We use the Medicine Wheel to transport us through time and space. To enter a "non-ordinary reality," or an altered energetic state to tap into sacred wisdom and guidance.

Stay with me!

When we enter a Medicine Wheel, it is with great intention to ask questions, request guidance or support, and dialogue with Spirit.

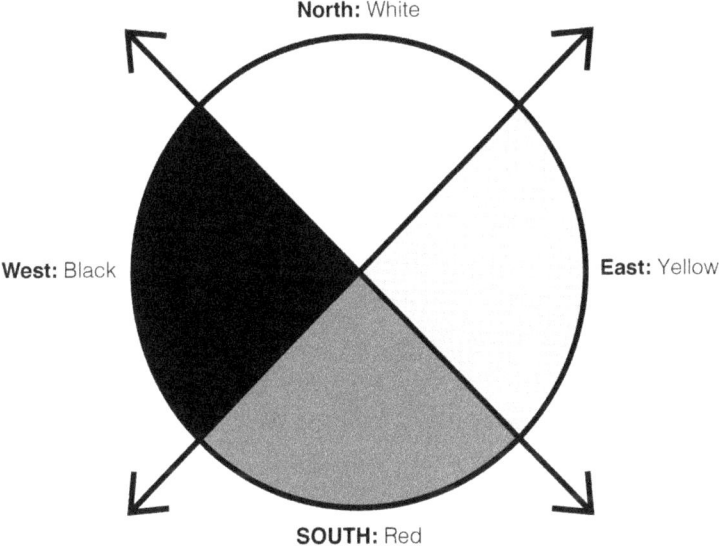

I chose which college to attend by doing a Medicine Wheel. I use the Medicine Wheel when seeking answers about relationships or complex projects. I go to the Medicine Wheel for ideas, and the more I connect to it, the more I settle into my own skin. One of my favorite memories happened one afternoon when Mom told us all to go out on the Earth, do a Wheel, and then come back to the house for dinner.

I packed up my medicine bag, took tobacco for prayers, cornmeal to mark the perimeter of the Wheel, and a notebook and pen to document my experience. After about an hour in the woods seeking guidance, I got back to the house excited to hear about everyone's experience.

As we sat down to debrief, Mom asked, "How was that? What did you learn?"

I started rattling off what each direction told me and shared my initial topic and question. Both my moms became quiet, and their eyes lit up.

Dreaming Bear gasped, "Whew! You got more in an afternoon than I get in a year."

That moment solidified an important piece I couldn't articulate: This was natural. Speaking with Spirit was one of my gifts.

It felt easy to go into the woods and ask for help. I didn't have any inhibitions blocking me or expectations of how it *should* go. It just was. Nothing more, nothing less. I didn't know it could be any different.

I felt a little self-conscious but also really excited because I found something special I was good at—listening to my Spirit Guides, hearing my inner voice, and trusting myself. This is one of the biggest differences I see in the way my moms raised me versus other kids. My moms acknowledged my gifts early on and nurtured them. I never shut down or shied away from claiming these intuitive experiences because my family always lifted them up and honored them.

This also led to seeing a clear pattern of women much older than me in the Medicine Circles who struggled to hear their inner voice. Their natural gifts from childhood were often criticized or shamed out of them.

When I feel extremely emotional or stuck and want to *move* into a new space, I learned to call on the powers of the South—the water element—to get back into flow with nature. Sometimes I go to a river or just take a shower with intention. This might look like letting the water run over my hands in the sink and asking for release and relief from emotional pain. We use the elements as guides and powerful support.

Each direction carries different medicine and teachings, which all come together to support us.

Even in English we say, "Look at that water baby!" or "Wow! She's fiery!" or "I love how grounded you are," or "How impressive, you pulled that idea out of thin air!"

All those sayings align with the four elements: earth, air, fire, and water. Within the Medicine Wheel, each direction corresponds with a natural element, color, season, and teaching. If you have studied a different tradition, please trust the placement that feels right for you.

Here is an overview of the Lakota Medicine Wheel:

Begin with an invocation or opening prayer facing the East, calling in Great Spirit and the beings who love us. Then turn and face the South to begin with calling in each direction's medicine.

SOUTH:
- Element: Water
- Color: Red
- Aspect: Emotional
- Season: Summer
- Phase of Life: Child

WEST:
- Element: Earth
- Color: Black
- Aspect: Physical (body)
- Season: Fall
- Phase of Life: Adolescent

NORTH:
- Element: Air
- Color: White
- Aspect: Mental
- Season: Winter
- Phase of Life: Adult

EAST:
- Element: Fire
- Color: Yellow
- Aspect: Energetic and spiritual
- Season: Spring
- Phase of Life: Elder or infant (death and rebirth)

After the opening prayer—facing East—we were taught to walk the Wheel starting in the South and move clockwise to the West, North, and end in the East, ultimately with the goal to stand in the center at the end and integrate all of what you've learned. Holding the teachings and guidance from each direction to join you and support you in standing in not just *the* center, but *your* center!

The Medicine Wheel helps to ground, guide, and give us access to deeper spiritual truths. I feel grateful to have been welcomed into this work that created such a strong foundation and still continues to teach me, which we will delve into in the next chapter.

7

East Child

I've been a seeker from a young age, almost like searching the Earth, my insides, thoughts, experiences, and feelings for pieces to the puzzle of myself, hungry for answers from within and from Spirit. What happened? What will heal me? Where do I focus to take me further?

At the foundation of Medicine Work lives this principle that our guides, allies, and intuition are all working toward the common goal of finding a sense of balance and harmony. Ultimately, when we find that quiet space within, we send out ripples of peace and energy—contributing to healing the planet.

I like to call the messages we receive "whispers from the Universe." Sometimes they're faint, other times loud and pointed, trying to get our attention. As I got older, I started to take personality tests like Myers-Briggs, the Enneagram, and DISC Strengths Finder Assessment to receive validating information from an outside source. Growing up with the Medicine Wheel, I learned who we are at our core often gets covered over with society's rules, our wounding, and limiting beliefs.

Luckily, there are ways to unlock and uncover our true selves. One of the most powerful aspects of Medicine Work for me is identifying my Home direction. Knowing our "home" helps us see patterns and deeper truths. It also reframes our strengths and challenges into manageable pieces of the puzzle that are all important and connected.

With Medicine Work, there is no destination. You can study new dimensions of the Wheel for an entire lifetime and still be surprised. There are infinite layers to explore!

However, unlike other personality tests, we don't take a quiz or answer sixty questions. We learn to identify our Home direction after several years of sacred work with the Medicine Wheel. An important tenant is: Everyone and everything lives within the Wheel. One Home direction is not better than another. And we can learn something from each person's Home or way of seeing the world.

There are many different kinds of Wheels, and as mentioned, the Lakota Teacher introduced us to at least one Wheel, a workshop that corresponded with the season, direction, and theme of the weekend. This particular Wheel really touched me because it helped put things into perspective and showed me where some of my gifts lived. It also showed me how I was different from my parents. My moms are both "South people," so sometimes we had difficulty translating our experiences to one another.

I love this Wheel because it feels whole and all encompassing. It focuses on your innate strengths, challenges, and opportunities to heal. It is also a tool for self-reflection that helps us see ourselves more clearly. You wouldn't, for example, say, "My Aunt is definitely a West person," even if she exhibits many of those characteristics. It would be up to her to explore the Wheel herself and then decide and claim her own medicine.

For some people, naming their Home direction is immediately clear, while other folks may need a longer discernment process.

Often, talking with people about how they perceive us can give insight we can't see for ourselves, especially if they can reflect on your personality, quirks, and gifts from childhood. Focusing on our younger selves can give a better sense of how we were before the world told us to change, twist, and conform to something different.

Shortly after being introduced to this concept, my Home direction came to me, almost immediately. I am an "East Child" and have been told this repeatedly since I was young. I'm a fire person in many respects and am constantly moving, shifting, and learning.

As an East person, I really enjoy connecting with energy. It makes me feel safer when other people are aware of the collective whole. Often, East people can sense the vibe of a group or a space from a distance. Without any information, their intuitive "spidey senses" are often alert. I've not met a ton of East people, and I grew up feeling both misunderstood and special because of this.

East people are often in movement, engaged in personal transformation work, and seek fast change. For a tangible example, imagine the difference between tossing a flower into a river and watching it meander and move around obstacles, getting stuck, continuing with the flow, and eventually making its way downstream. This is a very South way of being in the world.

However, with fire, if you tossed a dry flower into the flames, it will spark almost immediately, turn to ash, and instantaneously change forms. Once fire touches it, it spreads quickly and fully engulfs the object. This is a very East person way of meeting change. Know anyone who impulsively quits their job, moves across the country, and starts over fresh just to "see what happens?" They feel restless and may, in fact, repeat this pattern many times throughout their life because there is a craving for sweeping change.

When I fully claimed being an East person, so much of my life made sense. It felt like coming home. Not every East person will identify with every single trait, but in my experience, it helped give a form to some of my desires. Dance, movement, martial arts, and creative expression often nurture East people's inner fire. I rarely want to sit still, and it feels even harder to get my mind to calm down and settle. This is indicative of our place of Challenge and Healing, which we'll cover in a moment.

Two people could stand at the front of the room and give the same exact presentation, but their Home direction would inform how they see the world and, therefore, how they put together and share their knowledge.

For instance, our Lakota Teacher, a West person, filtered everything she taught through a West lens. West people tend to be, but not always, more introverted, feel comfortable diving deep into themselves for answers, and use physical exercise to feel connected. West people like going into their metaphorical cave of darkness. Spiritually, this translates to having access to a deep inner silence where they can access their soul's messages and retrieve wisdom from going within.

West people often like being alone with their thoughts and feelings. They may have a deeper connection to the Earth, enjoy gardening, or feel better when they're outside. Nature calls to them, but so do books or journaling. They are often self-reflective and more willing to sit with the unknown.

Mom was a South person, so she consciously and unconsciously filtered everything through an emotional lens with a focus on healing. As a therapist, she did a lot of work connecting people to their inner child and soothing the heart space. South people often sense the feelings of people around them. They connect with water and flow and enjoy having deep conversations. They can be both massively in touch or overwhelmed by their emotions—like getting stuck in a swamp of sadness. South people often wear their heart on their sleeve or, when unbalanced, repress their emotions because it doesn't feel safe.

Sometimes South people are the watery ones—tears come easily, or they're called "overly sensitive" (they're not!). They're simply in touch with their emotions and can often sense the feelings of people around them. They can be flowy in the way they dress or how they interact with time. They also may feel nourished by interacting with water, in the shower, swimming, or connecting with local bodies of water.

A close family friend, Julia, is a North person. She is very intellectual and accomplished in her craft. North people are typically very curious, inventive, and analytical. Their power comes from the mental realm and tapping into the brain space. They can be "thought leaders," coming up with new theories, systems, and designs. They are incredible problem solvers and rely on their intelligence. Often applauded for how much they achieve, they can be strong assets to companies. They may like spreadsheets and making order out of chaos. They like to read a lot and take in new information.

Incredibly inventive, North people have an internal drive and ambition to not just solve the world's problems, but they can also create solutions out of thin air.

As you read, you may notice identifying with more than one direction. The truth is we have all of this and so much more inside, but there tends to be one that feels more natural. Again, this is a more advanced Wheel that would often be introduced after a couple years of deep personal work, but it is a powerful one to read through and let wash over you. Notice how each direction's description hits you.

Once we identify our Home, we can then determine the rest of the Wheel—connecting with our place of Challenge, Wounding, and Healing.

Follow the pattern below: Directly across from your Home direction is your place of Challenge. Then, moving clockwise one direction to your right is your Wounding, and lastly, directly across from that is your Healing.

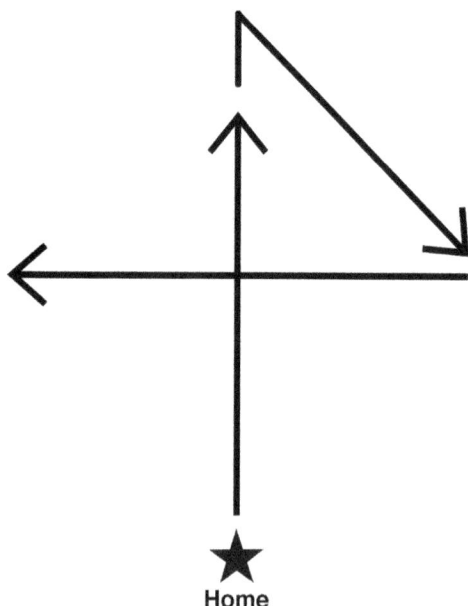

This is my personal illustration as an East person:

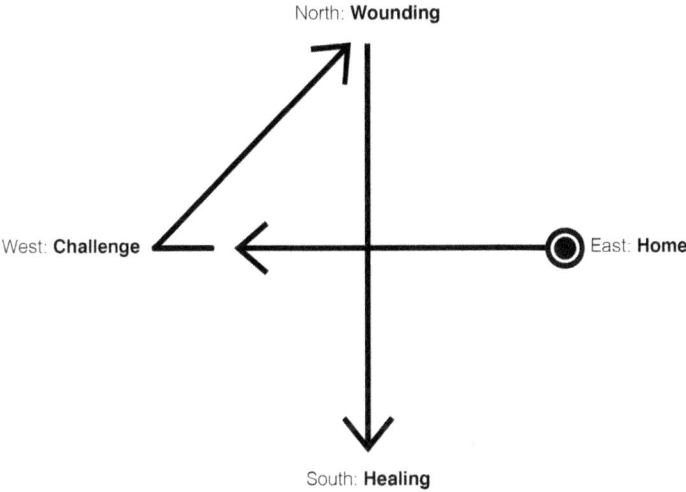

If your Home is West, then:
East is your Challenge (directly across);
South would be your Wounding (one direction to the right);
and North is your place of Healing (directly across).

Insights from this Wheel can feel incredibly validating. It helped me understand myself better as a whole.

Knowing I feel most at home with Fire and Spirit, I have a clearer pathway to handle my challenges and obstacles as they arise. As an East person, I am more comfortable connecting with energy, hanging out with the stars, listening to the wisdom of the ancestors, and playing in the energetic realm, both alone and with others. I learned to see people's energy, feel into it, work with it, and ultimately assist others with integrating and grounding their own energy.

Integrating energy and movement into all I do not only illuminated a strength of mine but also led me to discover more of what brings me pleasure and lifts my mood. My Home helped me discover a love of prayer, connecting to Spirit, and a desire to contribute to healing the energy of the planet.

You're reading a book full of teachings, lessons, and stories written by an East person. The reason I point this out is because I'm sharing information through a more intuitive and transformation-focused lens. If a South or North person were writing this, it would come across very differently. Knowing the Home directions of my Spiritual Teachers helped me understand more of where they were coming from and their own strengths and challenges.

It feels both revealing and freeing to share how this translates in my life.

East = Home:
Safe, comfortable, and where I anchor into to fill back up. Love playing in the mystery and energetic realm.

West = Challenge:
Whew! A battle often with my own body, physical health, and pushing myself to slow down and find stillness. Our place of Challenge can be both aggravating and extremely helpful. This is the place of "it may be good for me, but that doesn't mean I like it," i.e., meditation, working out, routine, and consistency.

North = Wounding:
For me, the mental realm feels unbalanced, often having swirling thoughts leading to anxiety, being ungrounded, scattered, and struggling with negative self-talk. This means I have accepted that while I'm smart, I can also get in my

own way. Our wounding is a good place to ask for help (i.e.: therapy or working with healing professionals). Finding support can create more balance and awareness, leading to a happy, healthier life.

South = Healing:
I love feeling my feelings! I enjoy talking things through with a good friend. Hearing heartfelt stories and connecting with the heart/energy of love feels so nourishing. It also leads me to connect with water—as simple as taking a bath—or doing ceremony at a river asking for support to "go with the flow."

Each direction has different qualities depending on whether it's your Home, Challenge, Wounding, or Healing.

Since I feel at home with energy, I actually have to be careful about not going too far out. When I do journey work or guided meditations, my energy might easily land in different realms of Spirit. I learned early on the importance of creating a container and connecting to the Earth both before and after exploring the energetic realm. This means tapping into that sacred West energy for grounding. You'll notice there's a good bit of grounding or body-oriented exercises included.

I have always felt more comfortable with the stars than the Earth—closer to energy than to humans; safer with nonverbal connection than words; dancing it out and following my intuition rather than intellectualizing my way through things.

You'll hear me repeat this phrase: "Your intuition is never wrong," never, ever, ever. Sometimes the interpretation can be off, but that gut feeling, or sense of knowing without rational information to back it up—that is always correct!

· · · · ·

I've noticed our gut feelings can guide us further, faster, and closer to soul-level alignment than anything else. Also, that is such an East person thing to say! I love talking about intuition and the intangible energy we feel because I would have loved to read something like that as a teenager. It would have given me an example of someone owning their spiritual gifts, even if words don't always fully capture the intangible.

In 2021, I met up with a friend in Atlanta I hadn't seen in a couple years. We texted every few months but hadn't caught up properly in a long time. She's an amazing dancer, and I asked if she would move with me at the park.

She had a meeting to get to, so we only had a few minutes. I set a timer on my phone. We both wore masks and sundresses in the August heat. We took off our shoes and stood in the grass. Twigs and sticks that had fallen from the trees overhead lay on the grass. We took a few steps back from one another so there was space to enter.

As professional dancers and improvisers, we were used to playing with contact and sharing weight, but I hadn't danced with someone in person in nearly two years. My friend Betsy is an incredible movement artist. She dances full time, and I always admire her work and presence.

Dancing with someone in this way, when you don't talk but want to explain something, is vulnerable and soul stirring. We took turns initiating and following. Just breathing and flowing in the moment. No words, just movement, energy circulating between us and "listening" with our bodies for the next move.

It was not choreographed, nor was there a specific destination or end goal beyond connecting. We just showed up and were present with one another. I cried from the sensation of conscious human touch in this way. It had been so long since I moved with someone who "gets it." Betsy was very responsive to the shapes I made, and I listened closely with my body to follow her. We leaned into one another—backs, hands, heads, calves touching, never stopping but taking a breath in certain positions to feel into what would come next.

This language beyond words is my favorite.

Once, in a spiritual workshop, the group talked about life purpose, and I declared, "Mine is to move and be moved by the world." It felt all encompassing, simple, and resonant. I often work off of resonance instead of words, listening to the in-between and feeling into the space to see what's there.

I know this language is unusual, so if these words are vague, I invite you to *feel* your way into them rather than try to figure them out with your brain.

The best part of this type of improvisation is there is no right or wrong way to do it. It takes a lot of body awareness and trusting yourself to share your whole body with a partner. It's intimate and fluid. You can't pretend to trust in these spaces or someone will fall. It gets too awkward and clunky.

Moving with the intention of sharing something without words is a beautiful way to connect with a person and their energy. This is another practice that fills my heart and reminds me I am whole, truly just an embodied spirit passing through time. I imagine Mom watching from the stars and saying, "There's my East child."

That day in the park, we moved slowly, twirling, leaping, and coming back to the Earth, engaging all the directions: East (energetic), South (emotional), West (physical), and North (mental). We took deep breaths of the air around us, danced with the unspoken energy between us, connected to the creative spark within, and cleansed with tears and flowing movement.

It reminded me: All of *you* is welcome here. Your Home, your place of Challenge, your Wounding, and your Healing. It takes all parts of us and all parts of the Wheel to create balance.

8

The Last Workshop

Almost every morning when I got out of bed, Mom sat on the sun porch reading a book with hot water and lemon. She started each day this way and mostly just wanted to be left alone until after she had coffee. She passed on a love of reading, and when I was a kid, she set a timer and gave me a book to dive into so she could dig into one of the things she loved most. She loved learning and taught me to appreciate many versions of wisdom.

She always had a "daytime book" and a "nighttime book," starting the day with learning and ending with fantasy or a novel to unwind. She dug deep into these two worlds and danced between them smoothly, desiring both the knowledge of the Himalayas and the magic of dragons.

Therefore, I lived between these two realms as well, detaching into the mystical realm of fiction and relating more to ancient wisdom traditions as I got older.

The event that catalyzed Mom's spiritual growth and development occurred after her initial diagnosis of breast cancer when I was nine. It's like the bottom fell out at that point. I didn't understand, and of course she shared some but not everything with me as a kid. While I don't remember a specific conversation about her path changing, I could feel it shifting. A new sense of urgency vibrated through our home. She really wanted to get through things by putting in the work, not just medically but spiritually as well. She approached her cancer healing from several levels simultaneously: blending Eastern and Western medicine and support.

Mom, always a seeker, deepened her commitment to her healing around the time she found shamanism, essentially making me her apprentice—in the traditional sense of living and learning together. We had always done rituals as a family, but they took on a different level of importance. Before I started studying directly with the Lakota Teacher, Mom began introducing teachings from workshops. I remember how things shifted—from general ways of connecting with nature to specific tasks and ceremonies. This continued to evolve as I got older and developed a deeper understanding and relationship with the Earth's medicine.

I went to public school, but Mom firmly believed you learn more outside of school than in, which my teachers didn't love. I was absent often. However, I maintained good grades, so Mom took me out of school regularly for "learning experiences."

What I didn't know at the time was that my family basically joined a Mystery School. Everything was kept extremely private and confidential. From time to time, the Teacher led larger workshops open to the community.

I attended one about connecting with your personal medicines, which is some of the foundational work of building a medicine bundle that serves you the rest of your life. Each item in the bundle connects the physical and energetic realm as part of the medicines we carry. We learned we each have a tree, a plant or flower, a color, and a stone that we are matched with this lifetime to learn from and connect with for guidance. Each stone, plant, and color has a different energy. It almost reminds me of a superhero learning about their powers.

The way you discover your medicines is through a shamanic journey. A journey is similar to a guided meditation, except you are actually connecting and traveling to a different place and time in the spirit realm. There are many different kinds of shamanic journeys. Some are led with words and others with music, drumming, or the sounds of nature.

The piece of this journey that impacted me the most was the search for our stone. As I tuned into the live drumming, my journey took me deep into a volcano. I could feel the heat as I envisioned scaling the outside and going over the edge. In this journey, I hovered above, taking in the imagery almost like a drone. When I entered the volcano, there was water at the bottom.

As I followed the trickle in the dark, I found a specific stone waiting for me where the water and fire met. This is a theme in my life, of balance and play between the elements. When we finished this journey, everyone in the group gave small tidbits of their experience. No one else had gone into a volcano. This makes me laugh because that is how I have learned to trust Spirit; over and over again, the answers I get are not ones I would consciously choose.

Finding our medicines, or our answers in general, is not about what we like or prefer but rather listening to a deeper connection between the energetic (divine) and physical (human) realm communicating.

After the journey, our task was to find a physical representation for each of our medicines. I think of this as a shamanic scavenger hunt, where I went everywhere from a grocery store to a craft store, walking in nature, and searching for pieces to symbolize and ground the energy. After I shared my experience with Mom, she gifted me a perfectly round lava rock from a volcano. It was so unique.

I use this stone to connect with my inner fire, mirroring the Earth's core. Walking between both worlds often includes anchoring the energetic and spiritual with the physical realm. Learning about my personal medicines was a huge gift. We also created medicine pouches to wear around our necks. Mine had a long braid and sat against my heart, so I could be conscious of and work with these medicines on a daily basis at first.

A big part of my healing lies in breaking the silence surrounding my spiritual practices. For many years, I didn't speak about it or share. It feels important to allow my spiritual self to have a voice.

Now I check in intuitively to see what feels right to open up about, doesn't break confidentiality, *and* honors my own experience. The isolation of this work felt rather jarring when I was younger. After years of studying with different Teachers, I now sift through what lives within me that can serve as a teaching for others and what needs to be kept private.

Mom left the original group and pursued further healing work and training. Ultimately, this led her to re-embrace her role as a Spiritual Teacher, where she combined therapy, shamanic healing work, and women's empowerment practices to support her students. I witnessed her growth from sharing teachings and exercises passed down to designing her own workshops.

She started to listen more to her intuition and merged it with her creativity. She would spend hours writing out new workshops and Medicine Wheels to teach. As I got older, she had me help her prepare for workshops by typing up instructions and gathering materials. I saw her gain confidence and trust in herself to receive messages and direction from Spirit.

Even though our journeys took a parallel path, I definitely had a different experience. As Mom started her own Medicine Circles of women, she allowed me to join when I turned seventeen. At that time, she literally became my Spiritual Teacher. This brought both gifts and challenges. I imagine it is similar to having a parent be a pastor at a church. There is a different set of rules and expectations, which led to a lot of resistance on my part, in learning from my mom. But it also gave me behind-the-scenes priceless access to this work.

For many years, Mom didn't call herself a shaman. In our tradition, this is a title that is earned over years of work and includes a "death and transformation of the self." Her cancer played a big part in this, and I had a front row seat to her personal and professional evolution.

Mom lived her dream of having her own students. Dreaming Bear provided the space and built cabins on her land in North Georgia for Mom's students to stay for workshops. We all played a part in supporting this dream.

Mom did powerful, lifesaving work—not because she directly "healed" or saved people, but because she created space for people to step into their power and save their own life.

I vividly remember Mom's last workshop. Her cancer had started to metastasize, and she wore some athletic tape on her arm to help keep the swelling down. She wasn't sharing much about the current condition of her health because she didn't want to scare her students. We gathered around a desktop computer to watch Brené Brown's TED talk, "The Power of Vulnerability," and afterward, Mom shared what she was going through (Brown 2010). This room, packed full of women, fell silent. Tears started to come for many folks, and I kept quiet. I knew they needed time to process, as I had been living with this reality for a while.

We were all a little squished together in the small room. Mom held space for people to respond, to ask questions, and then gently moved on to the topic she wanted to teach on, viewing vulnerability not as a weakness but as a powerful tool for connection. I watched Mom take up space in a sacred and powerful way. In her failing body, she shared her truth and honored what she came to do this lifetime.

Before the workshop, Mom said, "I came here to be a Spiritual Teacher, and the day I cannot do that, I don't want to be here anymore."

Unfortunately, I saw that come true. Shortly after Mom's last workshop, her cancer took over her whole body. She died a few months later, and I remember that sentence so vividly marking a turning point in her health. When we can no longer do what we were put on Earth to do, it's time to leave.

9
Searching for Acceptance

I grew up equating productivity with love. I thought the more I achieved, the more love I would receive. The systems in place even encouraged this. As a kid, I worked out a deal with Mom that for each A on my quarterly report card, I would get $1, for Bs I got $0.75, Cs $0.50, and so on. Looking back, this eerily mirrors a performance review as an adult, where your salary is tied to accomplishing or exceeding certain metrics, reinforcing the goal of high achievement early.

Anyone else fall into that trap? Society praises our accomplishments and encourages us to push further and further, solidifying the idea that more is better. More hustle equals more love. In general, society does not reward us for resting, taking care of ourselves, or exploring what lights us up when there is no gain. Mainstream culture does not reward us for simply *being*.

It feels ironic I've spent most of my adult life solely existing and fighting for that to be valued and honored—both within myself and in the world. For me, this relates to a powerful pull toward elder energy. It's something you can feel just by being around somebody. It's their presence more than anything else. I've connected with this energy since I was young. Being called "mature" or an "old soul" can be a sign of this.

Friends often came to me for wisdom or guidance, not because I had my life together, to be clear, but because I could hold space for people to hear themselves more.

So often, when we look for advice, we're actually seeking permission for what we already know we want to do.

In fifth grade, I thought the more I did, the more I would be liked. I participated in band, chorus, dance club, the gifted program, and gymnastics. Since I equated achievement with love from an early age, I saw that message drilled in over and over again.

I received praise because I was good at doing a lot. In my mind, the equation was simple. The more I did, the more love I would gain. Unfortunately, not everyone saw it this way. Toward the end of the school year, we were passing around yearbooks to get everyone to sign. You could see the little messages everyone wrote to each other. "LYLAS" (love ya like a sister), "KATS" (kick ass this summer)—you know, the deep profound messages fifth graders write each other to remember people they'll never see again.

Some kids would save whole pages for their best friend to write out a long, thoughtful note referencing their inside jokes and shared adventures. Some of the shyer kids had lots of blank space because they didn't want to go up to everyone and get their yearbook signed. One day in class, we were passing them around to sign. It was customary to find your picture and write a little note nearby. As I flipped through to sign, someone had circled a picture of me and written "Bitch" over my face. It was honestly the first time I'd blatantly heard of someone not liking me.

It certainly stung. Even writing this now, almost twenty-five years later, I feel the echoes of that betrayal rumbling in my stomach. It wasn't so much that this specific person didn't like me—truthfully, I didn't like her either. I was shocked to see it in writing. I wracked my brain and thought, *But I'm in chorus, and I get good grades, and I choreographed that gymnastics routine…* but none of that mattered.

We are not worth more because we perform more.

Our inherent value comes from the love we carry—and how we decide to share it with the world.

Of course, that is not a fifth grader's thought. That is a lesson learned over time with lots of unlearning and working to decouple productivity from self-worth. I was eleven years old, and already the capitalistic mentality was ingrained. "You're worth more when you do more."

In that harsh moment, I learned several important lessons:
- Not everyone liked me.
- In the future, not everyone was going to like me. (This is still a bummer.)
- Participating, churning out work, or constantly juggling multiple projects does *not* equal having a good personality.

Now, while that moment was heartbreaking and truly a turning point in how I learned to show up in relationships, I also will own the fact that I was a bossy child who valued self-expression and spoke up. Today, we jokingly call that "showing leadership skills."

Being a sensitive child, I got my feelings hurt easily. I do not have thick skin, and as an adult, I certainly do not belong to the trendy "No fucks given" club. I do, in fact, give many fucks, and I care a lot. I didn't always nurture my friendships as I have the last ten years. Growing up, I often looked to others for validation. I still do, but I found a certain internal compass along the way that guides me back to center. Of course, I don't always listen to that internal voice and am definitely not perfect or enlightened, but I am committed to my path.

That moment in fifth grade taught me how powerful friendships can be, because it was lacking. I started to honor relationships differently because they took mutual opting in. I knew I wanted to connect with people who wanted to connect with me.

That may sound simple, but this topic showed up in coach training in my early twenties. I kept showing up for relationships that felt imbalanced, feeling like I put in all the work. Finally, my coach at the time asked me, "If you were a kid, what would you have done?"

It slipped out like the most obvious answer in the world. "If someone didn't like me, I wouldn't play with them."

It's so simple. No pining over a relationship for four months—just a quick mental shift. "Ohhhhh—I want to play with you, but you don't want to play with me." Or, "You don't want to meet up at the park anymore. Got it, thanks! Have a good day." It could be that easy.

If we zoom out for a minute, our childhood selves often have great wisdom to share.

There is, of course, the caveat that our kid selves are not always meant to be in charge, making adult decisions, but tuning into your childhood self can help clarify your needs and offer a shift in perspective.

It's not the be-all-end-all answer, but it's something to consider. After consulting your Little Self, you can carry that wisdom forward. Each perspective helps us come to wholeness.

As an experiential learner, that moment in fifth grade foreshadowed how important relationships would be for me later. I honestly felt burned by my friends growing up, rarely experiencing fierce loyalty or standing up for each other. I could see the ways I failed to show up for others and the focus I had on *doing* rather than *being*.

I know I wasn't always the nicest kid, but this moment of being called out spiraled into developing some pretty heavy people-pleasing tendencies. That feeling of being on top of the world tumbled into some intense self-desecration. Ultimately, I learned to be kinder and place a lot of value on authentic connection. But that would come later. At first, I definitely tried to solve my self-esteem problem with a Band-Aid.

I had this sinking feeling I wasn't valuable unless I was producing. So, instead of getting to the root of the issue, I merely chose a new route to obsess over—being popular in middle school.

I wanted to be popular so badly because I thought it would solve my problems. If the right people liked me then I would be validated, valued, and safe. I wouldn't get made fun of. I would have a crew. And ultimately, I'd belong with the "right people."

After the yearbook incident, I really turned inward. Knowing people didn't like me and felt the need to memorialize it hurt. I wanted to belong no matter the cost. I just wanted to be liked.

Several days a week, I came home crying after school. I didn't know it at the time, but Mom called one of the other parents and told her what was going on and asked her to speak with her child about being kinder. It didn't help. Kids are mean. I was a mean kid for a time, so I've seen both sides of this coin.

Hankering for a best friend, I literally picked someone who lived near me and said, "Hey, I don't have a best friend. Do you?"

She didn't, so we started hanging out, watching TV after school and studying together for tests. As our friendship developed, I felt like I belonged more in the world because I had a best friend. For me, that meant acceptance. I wish that had been enough. As I saw other kids around us becoming more popular, I focused on social status.

I wanted new friends who could pull me up the social ladder. I thought popularity meant being admired, which would offer more safety. Quality friendship was certainly not the goal.

These experiences led me to truly value relationships and friendships today because of the way I devalued it when I was younger.

Trying to Fit In versus Authentic Acceptance

Then I did stupid stuff to "become popular."

I wore ribbons in my hair, created a notebook to pass around like a shared diary, and taught the cheerleaders a routine in the bathroom.

By middle school, I had joined the dance company, training five to six days a week. I didn't have time to explore many other interests. While most of my friends played sports, I could only play soccer at school during PE. Even though I was decent, I knew I couldn't pursue it further.

Dance made me different. I had to take care of my body around the clock while training to be a professional dancer in New York. I felt a lot of pressure and didn't really share my fears of not being good enough. I just sucked in my stomach and stuffed down my nervousness every time I put on a leotard and tights.

It felt a little like living a double life. Kids at school didn't understand the level of commitment I had, and the other dancers showed no interest in being friends. Tough social dynamics and inherent competition existed between us. So, again, I felt like an outsider.

I grew quiet. I didn't talk much because I didn't want to be embarrassed, which compounded my strangeness. Thus, my nervous system remained heightened almost all the time, and I really just wanted to get things right—in dance class, in school, and with friends.

Perfection would save me. My life would then make sense. If I were perfect, I'd be safe.

Unfortunately, there's no such thing as perfect, and while we're all trying not to be rejected from the pack and torn down, a large part of that acceptance has to come from inside.

I look back at my younger self and just want to say, "Oh, sweetie. This isn't worth it. They don't see you. They don't want to get to know you. And in a few years, you'll never talk to them again anyway. It'll be better in the long run to find people who like you for you, or to learn to like yourself." But we weren't quite there yet.

At the time, I would've rather been somebody else. My authentic self didn't seem to be winning any awards. I even had an adult tell me, "Be careful not to sell your soul for popularity. It's not worth it. And once you do, you can't get it back." I remember my body tightened, and I cringed at the fact they could see me shrinking, adapting, and contorting to fit in.

It was painful.

It didn't feel like it at the time, but the Medicine Wheel work saved me. This powerful practice strengthened my connection to my internal wisdom and taught me about interconnection and the inherent value of all living things.

It taught me to value my own inner voice, strength, and unique gifts.

In some ways, I felt these two worlds pulling me apart. It was a confusing time to have such conflicting priorities: fitting in versus focusing on authentic connection and self-expression.

Nowadays, I am so grateful the latter won out, but it took quite a journey to get there. As I started to get deeper into my spiritual training, I got more in touch with myself and, consequently, less and less mainstream. Authenticity and popularity seemed to be at odds with one another, at least in this middle school context.

Just before a field trip in seventh grade, these two worlds collided. I casually mentioned to Mom that sometimes I saw colors around people, and she told me to talk to the shaman about it.

I brought it up at my next session. The Teacher asked me questions about what I saw. I shared the images and general color palette I perceived.

She listened and then chimed in very matter-of-factly, "You are perceiving people's energy bodies, and certain colors are connected to different chakras. Each one has a different meaning. Depending on what you see, you can also see holes in someone's energy field, where there was a rupture or tear. Or if it's super luminous, it can mean they have a healthy and thriving energetic body."

I took notes about what each color meant, and after the session, I continued to do my own research as homework. Mind you, I was thirteen.

The next week at school, I thought this would be a great topic to discuss while waiting for the bus. I told my friends proudly, "I can see auras. They look like colorful eggshells around people. And everyone is different. They can change, but there's typically one color that's strongest."

"Prove it!" one girl exclaimed. I felt put on the spot and tried to sink into that inner stillness to feel into the energy. I wanted to perform well and told the small group what I saw, but something felt off. It felt exoticized, like a party trick rather than a sacred act.

At that moment, I felt unsafe and wanted to retract what I had shared. I didn't want to cheapen this spiritual experience or "show it off" to get attention. I wanted understanding and to connect with people who also wanted to explore the energetic realm. That's certainly not what happened.

This experience taught me to be more discerning in sharing my spiritual experiences. Looking back, this lesson had a profound impact. I started to notice when and where it felt okay to discuss these experiences. Unfortunately, at the time, it was a bit of a shock and served as a pendulum-swing moment that moved me from wanting to openly share this cool new thing with anyone to keeping these "weird" experiences quiet.

I want to learn all I can this lifetime and hopefully make it to the next level of the reincarnation video game. I learned young, with both my family and spiritual tradition, to value advancement on a soul level. It's always about learning lessons and moving onto the next. Many adults asked me when I was younger, "Why so much urgency?"

The answer came from a deep place. I want to grow, learn, and move forward, ultimately finding the gifts in the challenges. This experience taught me to slow down and find the right people to let in to that special and sacred space so we don't keep repeating the same patterns.

10

Spiritual Surprises

Anyone who knows me knows I love to pray. Over my food, around a table with friends, giving energy to the Earth, or even just a quick, "Please, Spirit, help me!" on my way out the door to a big event. I luxuriate in connection with Spirit. As an energetically sensitive person, sacred space really fills me up. I get tingly sensations, and visually, things start to shift and expand around me. I feel a sense of being part of something bigger than us that honors both our human and divine nature.

Leaning into Spirit is like a trust fall—a little scary but also a relief when you are caught midair. In leadership trainings, I've done trust falls standing on the ground, from a few feet higher off a concrete embankment and from a platform several feet in the air. No matter the height, I get nervous every single time.

My body feels constricted, and I tighten my grip—on myself, on the air around me, anything I can grab hold of. But ultimately, I lean back into connection. And each time, someone catches me. Thank goodness. If anyone has been dropped in this type of experience, my condolences, because that would definitely be traumatic. Leaning into trust and feeling held is a great metaphor for how the energetic and physical are connected for me.

I was taught we actually have four bodies to tend to, called the PEMS bodies, referencing the physical, emotional, mental, and spiritual realms. All need upkeep, care, and attention.

One way to care for the energetic body is to pray and connect in community. I haven't been part of a shamanic circle since leaving home, so I'm often looking for spaces that are open to other faith traditions. In college, I went to Quaker meetings for worship—entering into a quiet space of "expectant waiting," where we sit together in sacred community and tap into something beyond words, something magic. For me, this often includes an experience of being altered energetically, which can feel a little like being inside an impressionist painting.

Where the edges are fuzzy and start to blend together is where my energy merges with the air around me, reaching out and expanding beyond my body and into the room itself, connecting with the unseen luminescent field (aura) around each person.

When I'm in a room of people praying, no matter what their beliefs are, I pick up on a sense of *reaching*.

Reaching toward Spirit. Toward a calling. A quiet place inside that is like entering into an internal dwelling. A home. A space that is beyond thoughts but occupied with love and wholeness. It's warm here. But everyone's inner landscape looks a little different. The space we reach toward can also evolve and shift over time.

Right now, my inner heart space looks like a cozy home with blankets laid over the roof to soften the impact of the outside world. It feels so gentle and beautiful to be here. I see candles lit and smell freshly made cinnamon buns warming in the oven. My favorite! The floors are just a tiny bit heated, like at a nice spa, and the walls are sort of floating and can change depending on the size of room I want to occupy. It feels like the perfect place for me.

If you were to design a divine spot for you to inhabit and rest in, what image comes to mind?

It doesn't have to look like mine. It may be completely different—on a cliff overlooking the ocean or a fancy hotel where you don't have to do any work. There are no rules here. We get to play.

If you're feeling disconnected or having difficulty coming up with something… I like to describe connecting to Spirit like going to an internet café in South America fifteen years ago. I lived in Bolivia for a summer and taught dance at an amazing community arts foundation. There was no home WiFi back then, so in order to call a loved one in the US, I had to go to an internet café.

Skype was just becoming a thing, and people from all over the world would flock to these little cafés that seemed like the United Nations of customers. I would even travel across town, taking multiple modes of transportation—bus, taxi, and walking—to get to a café that had a stronger connection.

Sometimes the line had static, or the call dropped. To me, that's how it can feel trying to connect with Spirit. Even if you go out of your way to find a peaceful spot—depending on the weather, both inside your own head or literally around you geographically—the connection can come through clearly or be intermittent and distorted.

For me, being part of a spiritual community can help heighten the signal. When we're all tuning in together, we strengthen the signal. I've had to adapt to finding people I feel comfortable exploring sacred space with rather than only looking for shamanic communities that are harder to find. Over the years, I've had powerful experiences sitting in prayer with Christians, Buddhists, Jews, and folks of various spiritual backgrounds coming together in sacred circles.

As a world religions minor in college, I was in one of my East Asian studies classes when my teacher mentioned offhandedly during a moment of silence that "Quakers and Buddhists use silence very differently." Then he went on with the lesson.

That concept stayed with me because I'd never thought of it that way. We all pray, connect, and engage with Spirit differently. I'd had such negative experiences with Christianity growing up. I was always looking for sacred spaces that felt safe. For me, I often found it in the nondenominational silent spaces. We didn't need to connect or pray in the same way, but I wanted to step into a group of people interested in engaging in a spiritual practice.

I think the best way I can describe what makes something a sacred space rather than just a silent space is the presence of a *longing*, a heart-based desire to connect with Spirit.

When Mom prayed out loud during ceremonies in our backyard, I could feel the resonance of her words in my body, rippling energy of light through my chest or a sense of fire between my hands. Sometimes I would feel it underneath my feet or at the back of my head, slightly buzzing.

Spirit has always lived in my body. I learned early on I needed a container to direct and channel that energy. The

Medicine Wheel provided a structure and literal container to step in, to connect with Spirit on Earth.

I know each road to Spirit is different, but as many have said before me, the roads all lead to the same place: a divine connection with something beyond our human form… no matter what you call it.

A friend asked me last weekend, "Do you think *everyone* can connect with Spirit?"

"Yes! Absolutely," I passionately exclaimed. "I also believe some people are more attuned or open to building their intuitive muscles on a deeper level."

I feel like it's my job to listen to Spirit and hear when people's souls cry out with the same longing.

At the heart of my spiritual practice is listening.

Often, people ask, "But how do you know if it's your voice or actually a sacred message?"

I have two answers, with one I heard years ago in a spiritual seminar. The practitioner was answering a question along these same lines from an audience member. Their response was simple and to the point.

"It doesn't matter. Who cares if it's something you heard in your mind that originated from you versus a message coming from the Divine? If it feels helpful, use it!" I love that. It can be such a relief to not overthink things and choose to trust the message itself, no matter where it came from.

Secondly, since childhood, Spirit has spoken to me by giving answers I wouldn't have *consciously* chosen myself. The first time was a turning point in believing in all this "spiritual stuff." I was quite the skeptic and wanted proof, to see indisputable confirmation.

When I was twelve, after a few months of working with the Lakota Teacher, she invited me to do a power animal journey. I knew this was a big moment in my training, as we were taught your power animal would be with you for the rest of your life. There can, of course, be an evolution of the relationship, and other animals may show up as medicine guides throughout your life—but your power animal is a soul companion.

It's important to note, connecting with your power animal is a treasured relationship that is earned and developed, not just picked out because you like pandas, for example. I do want to point out that in pop culture, sometimes the phrase "spirit animal" gets thrown around inappropriately. A fan commented on a tweet, "Oh, Lizzo is my spirit animal!" to which Lizzo replied in a tweet from May 4, 2018, "The term 'spirit animal' is offensive to First Nation and indigenous tribes, but look, girl, I love that u feel like I'm ur inner self! *LOVE URSELF!*" I really appreciate the educational call out and redirection from Queen Lizzo herself.

As with the Medicine Wheel, there are also various approaches to power animal journeys in different cultures. This was my experience:

I closed my eyes as the shaman drummed and guided me into the realm of the power animals.

"Pay attention to the beings who show up." I had no idea what to expect. My moms had both done this journey before me, but they didn't share much about the process because they didn't want to spoil it. For weeks before my session with the shaman, I kept trying to envision who or what my power animal could be.

I imagined it would be an animal I liked and felt connected to—perhaps an owl, or a living version of a stuffed animal I had. I thought it might be a monkey, a manatee, or something else cute, but it wasn't. It wasn't particularly cute, pocket-sized, or predictable. It wasn't something I would have chosen. Instead, it felt like it chose me.

Before the journey, the shaman told me I would see my power animal four times or in four different facings (i.e.: head on = first time; sideways = second time). This instruction helped clarify in case I saw many different animals on the journey. I actually only saw two: a mouse that scampered by with an extremely long tail and a male rhinoceros. At first, I saw him from a distance and was curious but didn't want to get too close.

In the journey, I walked nearer and noticed this specific rhino only had one horn. At the time, I didn't know anything about rhinos, the different kinds, or where they came from in the world. The next time, instead of seeing my rhino, I felt him. He came up behind me and breathed on my neck. I get chills thinking about this even now, over twenty years later.

He showed up with masculine energy and was very playful. In the power animal realm, nature's laws, gravity, or behavioral expectations do not matter. This rhino would somersault and do headstands. He was very silly and, at times, also kept his distance, teaching me about boundaries, self-protection, and being appropriately guarded.

I asked permission to approach him, and he invited me to sit on his back. I climbed up and could feel my feet dangling off the ground with his height. I lay down horizontally and rested my full body weight on his back. Then I could feel myself sinking into his body, and we merged.

I felt the major weight change, and my feet stretched down into his hooves as our bodies melded. I felt the air gently whip across our faces as we started to walk and then pick up speed and run. We became one, and I was encased by his large form and could feel everything he felt. I didn't know why, but I trusted him completely. We shared vision looking out through his eyes, and I felt my body shift to the height of his statuesque figure. After that merging, we came to a clearing in the grass and separated. I moved back into my own form and sat with him to talk.

At this point, the shaman directed me. "Ask your power animal for a piece of wisdom to bring back with you." I asked if he wanted to share anything with me. Very clearly, I heard the words, "Know yourself." At first, I thought that was somewhat universal advice. But remember the context: I was in middle school and having a hard time truly being me.

This phrase ended up having a huge impact on my life, as so much of my personal medicine is about unapologetically being myself and knowing my truth. I thanked my rhino, offered him a gift in exchange for his wisdom, and left the spirit realm as we closed the journey. After a few deep breaths and fully regrounding back into my body in this time and space, I took some notes and debriefed with my Teacher.

I was shocked and giddy to receive my power animal, a lifelong companion and guide to escort me on my path forward. I remember feeling relieved and lit up, as this felt so real and tangible. I've connected with my rhinoceros many times over the last twenty-five years, and it still cracks me up this is the being who came to me. I never would have chosen a rhino.

My family used the book *Medicine Cards* by Jamie Sams as a reference when we wanted to look up the energy of animals. If we saw a turtle or a hawk, for instance, or had a dream with a bear in it, we'd look up the animal's medicine to learn more about the message.

Rhinoceros is not a common totem in this part of the world, so it is *not*, in fact, part of *Medicine Cards*. I was so bummed and started doing research to learn as much as I could. The one horn I mentioned is important. That made it specifically a one-horned Indian rhinoceros from Sumatra rather than the two-horned rhinos of Africa. As I searched for more information, Mom pulled out another book to reference titled *Animal Speak* by Ted Andrews.

There, toward the end of this book, was a small section on rhinos. Their medicine is about "ancient wisdom," which felt so resonant and aligned with being called "an old soul" practically since I was born. But this next moment took my breath away.

"[Rhinoceros] teaches how to be comfortable within yourself. They embody the mystery school axiom: 'Know thyself!'" (Andrews 2018, 309-310).

I gasped. The words stopped me in my tracks.

It pulled me back into the journey as I saw nearly the exact same words in quotation marks. Almost like a premonition, the words hung in the air.

This was the "proof" I'd been seeking. My body felt electric, expansive, and in alignment with my soul.

My spiritual journey often involves the element of surprise, giving me answers beyond what my conscious mind could come up with. I love that part. It teaches me over and over again to trust my inner voice and keep listening to what I know to be true.

11

Guided Meditation

Let's take a breath to let all of this sink in.
Sprinkled throughout the book, there will be guided meditations, tools, and exercises to help integrate and put what you're learning to use. *Please don't skip these.*

Embodiment is the way to truly absorb new information and explore what feels good and right for you. They will be labeled in bold: **Embodied Soul Practice** (ESP).

Think of this like an experiment. There is no right or wrong way to do this.

Now, if you're willing, take another full, deep breath, imagine the air moving all the way down into your toes then back up into your chest, letting it rise and fall. Don't worry about looking like a fool while you read this. I'm here with you.

What do you sense and notice in your body?

Embodied Soul Practice: Guided Meditation

I invite you to place your feet on the floor or Earth and read through this once so you get the process, and then, when you feel ready, close your eyes and see what shows up.

As you breathe and settle in, imagine a pool of glowing light beneath your feet. Notice if the light has a texture, color, or temperature. For me in this moment, it's golden. Yours can be any color you choose, or let it choose you.

Imagine the light seeping down into the Earth, calmly, deeply, moving through layers and layers of rock and soil. Reaching down into the center of the Earth. As you approach the center, find a soft spot where you can enter.

Do you move quickly, gently? Or you might choose to puncture it or slide through—this is all up to you. As you move into the very center, you are now engulfed in light, swimming in the same color from the beginning that was under your feet. Imagine it oozing over your body and wrapping you in the most amazing feeling you can imagine. Give over to this for a moment. Close your eyes and seep into it. See what it feels like to be saturated and surrounded by this light.

Before we leave this warm space of delight and love, there's something here for you.

Something personal just for you. It could be a word, an object, a symbol you're meant to bring back to the surface into your daily reality.

Search for it.
Call out to it.
Open your heart and maybe even your hands to it.
Notice if it wants to come with you easily or if there's resistance. If there's a clear picture or complete nothingness, both are okay.

Just allow your experience to exist and keep breathing—fully in and out.

Now, bring that special piece with you back to the surface, giving gratitude and blessings for your time meeting with the light, thanking it for showing up and enveloping you with love today. Know you can return here, anytime you need.

As you make your way back through the layers of illuminated Earth, notice if the temperature changes and what it feels like to move up to the surface.

Imagine reentering the pool of light underneath your feet.

Is it the same color from the beginning? Or has it changed?

Take another intentional breath here as you come back into your body. Take a moment to recall the object, word, or symbol you brought back with you from the center of the Earth. Envision holding it in your hands and placing it in your heart. Allow it to take up space, maybe even placing your hands on your heart if it feels good.

This can help calm your nervous system. Keep breathing and know you are being held and connected to something bigger.

And whenever you feel ready, no rush, gently open your eyes.

Come back into this space, and this time, waking up your muscles and bones, perhaps with a small wiggle or rubbing your hands together. I like to squeeze my thighs with my hands or trace the outline of my physical form.

My favorite yoga teacher back home would ask us to lick our lips when coming back from the final resting pose of class. The first few times I did it, I thought it was strange, but now it's one of my favorite ways to reenter my body after journeys.

Feel free to stomp your feet, stretch big, or get up and get some water. Take a moment to inquire about what your body needs. Now is a good time to pause.

Take a moment to be with what came up for you—when invited to connect with the light inside you.

You may want to jot down some notes, work with a candle, take a bath, go for a walk, set the book down, get up and move, or journal. I'll be here, along with your ancestors, teachers, guides, and allies, cheering you on.

We'll hold space as you dive deeper into weaving together what it's like for *your* divinity and humanity to dance together.

Congratulations, and thank you for doing this!

PART 2

12

Spiritual Teachers and Trusting Yourself

I don't know how to be an adult without grief. My entire adulthood seems centered around Mom's health journey, losing her, and rebuilding a life in her absence.

I lost my spiritual community the same time I lost Mom. Her students continued to meet for about a year after she died, and then, organically, they disbanded. This secondary loss felt incredibly tender, devastating, natural, and confusing all at the same time.

At the beginning of 2023, I participated in a local shamanic journey circle in Colorado. When the leader of the group introduced herself and shared her background and how she came to this work, she said something that stayed with me.

She said, "I've never had an *agreement* with a specific Teacher, the way most indigenous Teachers do with their students." This simple distinction made so much sense, yet I had never heard it stated so clearly. It felt so validating as to why I resonate with certain Teachers and feel uneasy with others.

It really blew me away. *Agreement* is the word I couldn't encapsulate before then. I've said things like dedicated or committed, but agreement goes both ways. We both have to step into the relationship.

I have had several agreements with Spiritual Teachers and, at this point, have lost two of my three main Teachers. I didn't realize other people weren't making that commitment on a yearly or quarterly basis within their spiritual community.

Each Teacher and lineage does it differently, and with our Lakota Teacher, we had to "submit" a prayer bundle with tobacco as an offering each year. Then the Teacher either chose to accept it or not. This determined how you proceeded with your studies within the Medicine Circles.

After Mom started teaching, and within a few years, she led an advanced healers circle. There was a commitment ceremony where each person had to stand up and speak.

I almost didn't stand up and could feel myself shaking. Mom and I had a conversation before the workshop. "I'm not sure I can make that commitment," I said. The advanced group involved twice the number of workshops in a year, working privately together, and investing more time, money, and energy than being a regular student.

"I won't force you. Of course, I want you to, but if it doesn't feel right, I understand," Mom replied. I saw a flicker of disappointment cross her face, but working with Mom as my main teacher was complex. I always had a bit of resistance.

I did end up joining the more advanced group. Unfortunately, shortly after, Mom's health started to decline.

My third Teacher, Don Mariano, had quite a different way of making a connection and commitment. In one of the workshops I took with him, we focused on deepening our relationship to the Apus (mountain spirits). He pulled out his *lineage stone* and asked us each to bring up a stone that would represent and hold that energy for us. As he performed the initiation, he linked his ancient lineage from the star beings, his ancestral Incan bloodline, and invited us to join his sacred family.

I wept as I felt the energy transfer from one stone to the other. We would now be forever linked. It was powerful and felt like a woosh of current running through his hands into the stones and into my hands holding my stone. Still, years later, I can hold that stone and feel the flow of energy anchored to his sacred lineage. This moment was one of sacred acceptance, belonging, and finding my place here on Earth.

The convergence of these two spiritual paths feels like it meets in my heart and moves down through my feet into the ground. Instead of feeling trapped between the human and spiritual realms, the merging of the Lakota and Q'ero teachings within my own body feels purposeful.

Since Mom passed, the last five to ten years have been an experiment in claiming my own gifts as a Spiritual Teacher and integrating what I've learned over the last twenty-five years. I will always be a student and continue to learn, take workshops, and explore new ways to connect with Spirit.

Much of that process is internal at this point, intuitively listening to the pushes and pulls of opportunities around me. A lot of my spiritual context involves connecting with the ancestors, both through my personal lineage of people I knew directly who have passed on and the star beings or greater ancestors who are accessible to us all. They show up to support, teach, and continue a living legacy from the spirit realm.

I want to offer a simple way to explore your own connection if this resonates with you. One aspect I love about shamanism is, while there are teachers and more experienced guides, every single person has access to Spirit.

We can all be messengers.

Simply meaning: We can both receive and share messages from the Universe.

When we tune into the interconnected system of wisdom that exists within all living beings, we have access to an incredible amount of "medicine" or teachings all around us.

Embodied Soul Practice: Discernment

Let's dive in together.

This is a simple practice to embrace your power to discern what you feel drawn toward or repelled by.

This practice can apply to everything from choosing which foods you want to eat to who you want in your life. You can use this to make decisions about jobs, relationships, see if a spiritual concept you're curious about is a good fit, and so on.

I invite you to sit right now, in this moment, and allow your body to breathe and relax. The invitation is to adjust and get 2 percent more comfortable. Imagine a small anchor hanging from your heart down to your gut like a pendulum. Notice with this image if it's moving, perfectly still, or wildly swinging. If it feels good, give your anchor some weight so it feels solid.

This may be unusual, but now is a good time to go with it anyway.

As you sit, imagine the anchor settling into stillness inside of you, running through your heart and into your gut. Now experiment with it swaying forward toward the front of your rib cage—passing through the center—and swaying back to your spine. Play with this a few times, just to experience the difference between internal movement and stillness.

Now let's create some meaning.

Imagine if it sways to the front, it's moving *toward* something you desire—yes.

Or lands back in the center in a neutral space.

Moving to your spine means it's moving away—no.

Listening to what *your* yes and no feels like today. For some, your yes and no may always stay the same, but I like to make space to check in and ask my body to give me clear guidance each time.

Envision a donut in front of you… or one of your favorite treats… What does your body immediately do?

Do you notice wanting to move toward it—desiring it—or leaning back and away from it?

Maybe you have dietary restrictions, and gluten and sugar aren't the best for your system, and you shift backward.

Or you just ate and aren't interested in dessert right now, moving more toward the center—a neutral space. No real emotional charge or attachment coming up here.

That central space can mean you need more time to decide or it could truly be a neutral response—both yes or no *could* be correct—but, right now, staying in the center could mean you need more time to make a clear decision. If that feels true to you, it might be a good moment to pause and pay attention. Don't push it. Usually there's a natural shift toward or away from something. Be patient, and let yourself be here.

Simply listen and allow.

Most questions have one of three answers:
- Yes
- No
- Not right now

The trick is to make space to hear your body's response and trust the knowing that guides you.

We start with a donut or whatever food you want to imagine because it's a lower stakes topic.

Now think of a topic you have a question about. Envision placing it in front of you and see how your body responds. Examples include: a relationship, job, potential risk, or big choice you have coming up.

Do you lean toward it? Stay in the center? Lean away?

What meaning do you make up about that?

I know this language can be a bit unusual, but slowing down to notice which stories start tumbling into your brain can be very helpful in the discernment process.

Like, *Oh wow! I didn't know I was so clear! My body is having a bigger response than I thought.* Or, *Wait… I'm not really hearing anything yet*, which is also a great answer. Give yourself more time to play with this new idea. You can even set it aside and come back when you feel ready.

Just listen to yourself for a moment. Suspend disbelief and give yourself some credit for trying it.

You know your own answers. Your body can be attuned to hear the subtle shifts and lean into your natural response.

Thank you for taking a chance and playing in this space!

13

Anxiety and Surrender

When I was anxious, Mom would tell me to go lie on the Earth. She said it so often it became a running joke with my friends. When I was going on and on about assignments in college or my latest love interest, my friend, Emma, would interrupt and lovingly, but annoyingly, ask, "Have you laid on the Earth today?"

"No, *Mom*, I have not. Ugh."

"Well, will you?" She'd shake her head.

"Fine." I know it's good for me, but it takes quite a lot to get me there. I think that's part of what's so funny to me about moving into a spiritual career. My experience with dance took a similar path; I really didn't want to turn into Mom. She had an undergraduate degree in dance, a master's in counseling, became a therapist, and then a Spiritual Teacher. When I was younger, I was determined not to follow that same path. I would say Mom was very "weird out loud," and I tried for years to keep my weird tucked away. Unfortunately, I didn't do as good a job hiding it as I thought.

Mom's taste in music was so unconventional. She listened to World Music, ambient sounds, and Celtic drumming, while I listened to top forties on the radio, inching toward the mainstream world as much as possible. She listened to Native American flute music during journeys, and I made mixes of Sean Paul and Tracy Chapman back in the day.

In college, I choreographed every semester, and after a couple of years playing with various kinds of music, I hesitantly selected a piece Mom used for meditation. It was theta waves that sounded like rain. The piece was so well received it brought the house down. Both surprised and honored, I chose to lean in. Further and further.

We've heard the trope in movies, "The worst thing in the world would be to become my mother." I feel like I made a complete one-eighty and ended up wanting to hold on to as many similarities as possible. Of course, had she not died when I was younger, that may not have been the case. But shifting from resistance to acceptance of our similarities is one of the many impacts of grief that turned my world upside down.

I remember hitting a wall in college my senior year. Exhausted from studying and losing sleep for more fun reasons, I knew I needed to regroup, and headed to nature. I packed a ground cloth, prayer ties, tobacco, and a clear intention for healing and releasing the constant worry I was feeling. I chose a stick to hold prayer ties, and as I left the apartment, one of my roommates looked me dead in the eye and said, "You think a stick is going to fix your anxiety?" She laughed, and I turned red with embarrassment.

She didn't understand. But she also didn't ask.

I walked past the last dorms and into the woods surrounding campus. Luckily, we had access to North Carolina's lush overlapping canopy, shade, and wide-based trees.

After I walked far enough on the path beyond where many people went, I laid the ground cloth on the Earth and got out all the pieces for my ritual. I always take a compass when I do Medicine Work because I have zero sense of direction and want to properly pray to the four directions.

I removed my shoes and called Great Spirit into the Wheel to help me heal and calm my energy. I lay down on the blanket, my legs sticking out from under my sundress, ensured there were no bugs wanting to crawl up my skirt, and then closed my eyes.

It took a while for my heartbeat to settle fully into the moment. My thoughts swirled as I dropped my hands by my sides and intentionally flipped them palm down to help with grounding. Calling in the energy of *Pachamama* (Sacred Earth Mother in Quechua), I prayed for Her to hold me and to know it was safe and okay to relax.

I felt my ribs start to heave up and down unsteadily with my breath as tears streamed down my face. There is a reason I don't love the silence and getting quiet. I don't always like what I hear in that space. It's where my overwhelm seems to live.

I turned on my side and pushed into the Earth. *Hold me!* I thought rather loudly.

I'm so tired. I don't know how to keep going, my internal monologue continued.

"Do you need to cut anything out?" I heard as Spirit's response.

"I can't," I whined. "I have to keep up with school work, volunteering, classes, dating my girlfriend, etc. I don't feel like I can let anything go at this point."

Just as I did as a kid, I instinctively began talking to Mother Earth, searching for answers in nature like Mom taught me. She used to talk to the flowers in her garden and made it look so natural. So I talked to animals, my dolls, and plants as friends when I was a kid. That continued into adulthood and shifted from playing to interacting with the environment, except I didn't really know other people who communicated with the world around them in this way.

As I grew older and began having bigger life questions, I turned to nature for guidance on certain subjects. Nature helps me calm down and go inside to tune out all the noise and listen. I learned I can ask nature or Spirit for support. I may not always get an answer, but I know it's okay to ask. The responses I get are usually short, simple, and direct.

If the answer starts getting too complicated, or I am fighting myself internally, I know I've gotten in my own way. Spirit speaks to everyone differently, and over time, I've learned Spirit speaks to me with images, feelings, and messages. I feel information come through my brain and move through my body. This serves as a check-and-balance system. One is not better than the other, but they work together.

Depending on the message coming in, I either tighten up or feel warm and expansive. Sometimes the elements show up as support, like water flowing as a healing energy or fire for cleansing, earth for grounding, and air for opening to new possibilities. These are generalizations, as there is nuance with the elemental medicines, but overall, this understanding is a good place to begin.

When I'm feeling stuck, sometimes I will just take a moment, go outside, and look at the sky, take in the clouds moving so far up above, take a breath, and remember I am not responsible for the clouds and, truly, "the clouds don't care about your problems."

That message came through clearly one day, not in a vicious way, just in a "Girl, breathe! Whatever you think is the end of the world truly isn't. The clouds will keep passing overhead, the weather will shift, day will turn to night and night to day again and again," the Universe seemed to say.

I appreciated the reminder I'm not the most important thing on the planet, both individually and at a more macro level, remembering humanity is not the center of existence. It's humbling to embrace the "speck of dust" perspective where we zoom out and acknowledge we're all floating on a giant planet hurtling through space and time—without truly knowing how our souls came into existence.

At the same time, whenever people say, "Will this really matter in ten years?" As a person who deals with anxiety, my answer is almost always, "Yes! I remember getting a B on an exam in fourth-grade language arts class. That tactic won't work on me!"

"You won't even remember that in ten years," a teacher said to me.

But guess who did?

Yeah, that's right. Out of spite and to prove a point, I held on to that because, obviously, that specific fourth-grade test score helped determine my entire academic path and which college I got into. *Don't try your helpful head tricks on me, teacher. I'll hold on to it and integrate it into my neuroses solely because you said it didn't matter. Thank you very much.*

You can see the reason I need an embodied approach to managing my anxiety and life in general. Whenever Mom told me to lie on the Earth I would grumble, but nine times out of ten, I found it incredibly helpful. I know there are scientific reasons why it's calming—something about the ions settling and connecting with organic matter and not looking at a screen helps the body de-stress. It's also the essence of unplugging and tapping in.

Because of how I grew up, going places with no service is one of my favorite, most calming things to do, when you have no choice but to stop searching for a cell signal and instead find a Spirit signal.

Sometimes when I lie under a tree in secluded woods, I can fall asleep on the Earth. That may not sound miraculous, but anyone who has a hyperactive brain knows relaxing to this degree can be life-changing. This memory lives in my body from when I was a teenager. I would venture out and find a nice rock to sleep on up at Dreaming Bear's. I often had small magical dreams and felt warmed by the sun, rejuvenated by the ability to feel safe enough to completely let go.

There was never any pressure in the woods. It was a safe place to land and let my guard down. As I slept on the Earth, it felt like the exhaustion drained from my body. I didn't have the energy to hold back or try to look good. I drooled a bit on my arm that day and woke up a little groggy. The temperature had shifted a bit, even though I was only asleep for about twenty minutes.

It was the desperate kind of sleep where I just couldn't hold myself any more. I needed to fill back up in a different way and start the day again. I opened my eyes and sat up, ready to pray into the Earth.

"I need you with me," I whispered. "Please. *Hampuy hampuy.*"

Hampuy hampuy is a phrase used by Andean priests to call the spirit of a person, god, teacher, or nature being. This phrase blends *hamuy (come in!) and hampi (spirit medicine)*, used at the end of a prayer or oration to anchor in the presence and medicine of the addressed spirits (O'Neill 2014).

I could feel some of the depletion in my body leaving, my muscles relaxing, and my eyes beginning to shift into soft focus. Sometimes this way of looking at the world is referred to as "seeing with your third eye." In this altered state of consciousness, I lean into the *feeling* of the world around me rather than holding a hard focus on any one specific object.

I prayed to expand and feel Spirit with me. I prayed to let go of so much worry and rigidity. I could always feel my body tense when trying to control the outcome. I needed to release into one of my least favorite spiritual practices: surrender.

Some of my spiritual teachers had attempted to teach me about surrender for a long time. But I think my resistance goes back to one of my favorite phrases as a toddler: "Self do it!" I would exclaim this regularly when Mom tried to help me buckle up in the car seat or tie my shoes once I knew how, even if it would take me half an hour.

Surrender, the opposite of control, involves *allowing*. For me, it often looked like closing my eyes and going with the energy of what was happening. When I can't see, I feel more into my embodied nature and start to listen with my other senses.

I kept hearing I needed to surrender—which is not particularly easy and can feel like being asked to "simply jump off a cliff." So, instead, I prayed, "Please, Spirit, give me *steps*. I have to break it down and take it slow. Show me how to let go little by little."

I have gotten better at it over the years, but sacred surrender is still not my absolute favorite—even though when I manage to truly give over, it feels heavenly.

Since I learn things best by including my body, I actually experienced the concept of surrender at a local creek in Atlanta. One day, I felt exhausted, stressed, and overwhelmed. I went to a place Mom called "the Watershed." This is not its official name, the park is not called that, no one else knows this spot by that name, and there isn't even a big waterfall or dam there, which makes me laugh. But we called it "the Watershed."

After a big rain, I headed down to the river. The water was high, and I was fully dressed. It was a slightly hot day but not terrible by Atlanta heat standards. I took my shoes off and stuck my toes in the water to test it. It felt good, so I looked around, made sure I couldn't see or hear anyone nearby, and decided to strip down to my undergarments.

Usually a pretty modest person, I just felt pulled to get in the river. I waded out farther than I had before, and there was a small current. Giving myself to the count of three to adjust to the cold water, I ducked under and got my hair wet, and then, instinctively, I lied on my back and started to float.

I had my eyes closed but noticed I was naturally drifting. Opening my eyes, I saw the most beautiful sky above and just felt my body going with the flow. It only took a few feet to feel the delight of being carried by something other than my own doing.

It felt luxurious and exciting to let go to this degree. I felt myself shake a bit in the cold water but got my feet under me and walked back up the creek to go again. Floating was one of the best feelings, especially since I was immersed in all the elements: the earth beneath me, the water around me, the air above me, and the fire from the sun shining down upon me.

"I did it!" I giggled to myself and couldn't wait to share this experience. It really felt otherworldly to let go. It finally clicked; surrender felt simple and good. I knew it could also be scary, but I found a way to gently go with the flow, literally; to just be gentle; move slowly; go where I'm pulled and trust the timing.

I needed to learn these life lessons using every fiber of my being. It's not a concept to just digest intellectually.

Our bodies serve as one of our biggest teachers and tools for integration.

> *Integration of the body can often be the missing piece. I've heard people say "Somatic healing is life-changing!" In my experience, there's nothing else like it. Integrating the body can mean the difference between "information and transformation."*

It gives new concepts and healing a place to land and settle inside us. Integration means something cannot be taken away or lost in the future. It's a part of us we will carry forward.

14

Sharing Energy

Growing up, I often felt like I lived a double life. In spiritual spaces, I was one way, and at school, I was another. Everything was far from integrated then. After being hurt by sharing some of my sacred experiences at school, I learned to keep them to myself. I inadvertently felt some pressure to "decide" who I was in each space. I didn't really have people my age who understood.

On weekends, I was off having magical experiences at workshops and then coming home to do math homework and go to dance class. I learned to keep these lives separate. As an only child, I spent a lot of time with adults. I was lucky enough to know someone else my age who believed in energy and nature's magic. We walked different spiritual paths but crossed over enough to have a shared language of mystical experiences.

Joel and I actually grew up together. We went to the same after-school programs for several years, and our parents talked. He was a couple years older than I was, and I had a huge crush on him. We would go back and forth about being boyfriend and girlfriend or just friends.

There were periods where we played together after school. Sometimes we were best friends, but as we got older, he became "too cool" for me. He abruptly stopped hanging out with me when he went to middle school and I was still in elementary school. Looking back, I get it. Even if it wasn't handled with the best communication, it was a natural boundary to make at that age. I was still fawning over him, though I seemed to stop existing in his mind.

Then, in a strange twist of fate, we reconnected years later and went on a date. Since we'd been close when we were younger, it was an interesting mix of shared memories and teenage hormones, creating an entirely new reality. In some ways, it was like we were meeting for the first time, and in other ways, there was a familiarity like coming home.

"I can pick you up Saturday at six p.m. Does that work?" Joel asked.

"Sure. Where are we going?" I wanted to plan accordingly.

"A surprise!" he said.

On our first date, he took me to a nature spot I'd never been to, with vines hanging crisscrossed from trees and ivy spilling over the Earth. I walked behind him on the trail a little confused. This land was back behind a house and didn't have a proper name on the map. It was a protected area that ran a little wild. My mind was elsewhere as we walked. I wanted to go to a movie or out to dinner. I didn't know why he brought me there.

I crossed my arms and felt closed off, not wanting to touch anything. I didn't like getting my hands dirty or dealing with bugs. In general, I like looking at nature but don't enjoy being engulfed in it. When we got to a concrete landing that jutted out near a creek, Joel turned around with a big smile on his face and said, "I thought you would like this. The energy here is really cool."

I looked at him hoping I missed something and tried to hide my disappointment. I could tell he saw a longing in me for connection: to a person, to something bigger than us, and to nature. It felt uncomfortable to have someone see a part of me I wouldn't truly recognize and claim for several more years.

So far in my life, I'd only shared sacred spaces with a group of older women, typically in their fifties. I wasn't used to sharing my energetic connection with anyone outside of workshops.

I also didn't know anyone else who went on dates in the woods. It felt so intimate and reminded me of that *feeling*, that old soul connection that couldn't quite be captured with words. It felt like awe and abundance and scary-exciting rolled into one.

After wading through the vines and starting to let my guard down, we went to an open field in a park nearby. It was getting late, and I had a strict midnight curfew. We talked and flirted from afar but didn't get too close, swinging next to him or sliding down poles on the jungle gym. I felt rather timid at first to talk about energy, especially since he said he could see it too.

On that humid Atlanta summer night, Joel and I stood in an open field. I had begun to let my guard down, but the mosquitoes, out in droves, kept biting us. It was annoying. But an idea came to me to open a dome of protection surrounding us. It felt like I could share this and we could play in this space.

He didn't have the words, but we shared an incredible night that would influence the rest of my relationships going forward. Not just romantic ones but also friendships, energetic exchanges, and a newly sparked desire to include spirituality in how I related to people in general.

I stood in front of him and called up some energy from the Earth, pulling it up above his head, and gesturing to extend it around us like a parachute, reaching down to the Earth and closing off the dome, guarding our space. I walked around in a circle to create a perimeter and asked him to call in the energy of the night sky and create a shield around us.

"It worked!" he exclaimed, jumping up and down a little wide-eyed and excited. "No more mosquitoes!"

"How strange and awesome!" Since I hadn't shared energy with anyone my own age, I didn't quite know what to expect. We met in the middle and hugged for a long time, just standing silent. I felt like my heart was going to jump out of my body.

We leaned slightly away, and I felt his hands reach above my head and come together to form a circle—which he draped over me and moved down around my back. We weren't touching; it was just energy. I joined my hands behind him and moved energy up his back and over his head.

It was like undressing with clothes on. I felt naked, like he could see me—hear my thoughts, fears, and desires. It felt raw and beautiful to be together in this way. We stayed in each other's energy fields for a few minutes, moving hands around each other, never touching.

"Can you feel that?" I asked when his eyes were closed, and I stood behind him, moving energy down his back, over his heart, and down to the Earth. We didn't use many words but stayed quiet, listening and leaning in.

Then we laughed and hugged again. I could feel my body shaking as we slowly pulled away and took so many deep breaths. Then, as we stood cheek to cheek, we kissed.

I knew this person. I knew his body that had lain next to mine watching stars as a kid in sleeping bags. We used to play four-square until Mom came to pick me up after school. He learned to play piano, and I sat beside him on the bench singing "A Whole New World," invoking a Jasmine and Aladdin scene.

It felt like we belonged to each other at that moment. It was me, him, and Spirit. Energy coursed through our veins, and the Earth shook slightly.

We leaned back in and held each other for a moment. Noticing the darkness around us, he checked his watch—11:42 p.m. He had to get me home.

Nervously, we leaned away. I didn't want that moment to end, but I also didn't know how long I could maintain it. We unwound the energy, releasing it back to the Earth and the Sky, thanking it for holding space for us that evening, grateful the mosquitoes left us alone long enough for this incredible energetic exchange to take place.

Then we ran to the car, both a bit bewildered by what had just happened. This was my first kiss. I was pretty disappointed after learning this was not how every kiss for the rest of my life would be. And, actually, this would be the only one that ever happened this way. It felt magical to share energy and intimacy.

The connection, layers, and power that opened up between us—with the Earth, within my heart, and honestly as a whole—really blew me away.

We made it back to my house with only two minutes to spare. He walked me to my door. We casually kissed goodbye, and I walked inside, closed the door behind me, and turned around. I put my hand against the door and smiled. I walked quietly to my room, trying not to wake Mom or have her come in and check on me.

I put my hand on my chest to remember to breathe. "*What?*" I asked the air excitedly around me. My cat was on the bed fast asleep. Used to hearing my stories, I told him what happened as I sat up wide-eyed in bed.

Well, that was fantastic! I thought. Sharing energy with someone my age felt incredible. It opened up a whole new world and initiated a longing and desire that would take years to fulfill again—linking intimacy with energy exchange.

We did not go on another date. Years later, we randomly crossed paths again and awkwardly recounted the story. I learned he called it an "explosion of energy." As great as it was, he told me it kind of scared him, which is understandable, especially since it was so rare. But I found my love language—sharing energy. Playing together in a sacred space after finding someone who already had knowledge and experience with Spirit.

This level of intimacy and sharing has only occurred a few times in my life, and I will forever be grateful it started that night—organically, through a safe and trusted connection. We bent space and time for a few moments, experiencing "spiritual love" together.

15

Loving Movement

Two of my early dance memories foreshadowed how I would relate to dance for years to come. At the age of five, I began taking ballet lessons. For our final recital, each student wore a tutu. Since this was my first time ever wearing one, I was off-the-charts excited! I focused on the frilly skirt, and our leotards, each decorated with a big sequined star, made me so proud that I kept watching the little light fairies dance around the room as the sun caught the sequins.

As five-year-olds, we did a routine that involved following the teacher and galloping around the space, waving at our parents, who sat in folding chairs on one side of the dance studio. But shortly after that performance, I quit dance. I kept getting in trouble in class because I just wanted to twirl. I didn't want to do the choreography. It felt limiting. I wanted freedom to move in a way that made my body feel good. That meant more to me than looking a certain way or being in sync with everyone else.

"I got in trouble for twirling" is about as true a "Meg moment" as can be. Self-expression is often at the core of what I want to do. Fitting in or following directions didn't worry me. I wanted to explore and enjoy the whole studio space.

I danced for that one year and gave it up. I didn't take dance class again until I was eleven because I associated it with restriction. "Do this, exactly this way" wasn't very fun, so I stopped. I wish I carried that level of permission forward in my life, but the next time I started taking class, I got sucked in and joined the dance company that trained five to six days a week.

Before going into my preprofessional experience, I want to dive into this second memory, which is one of my all-time favorite experiences of moving and being in my body.

In second grade, I went to Julia's Camp, an after-school program for elementary kids. She also ran summer camps and would pick us up from school in a big yellow van. One year we actually got to help decorate the van by gluing on knickknacks and painting our handprints on it. I loved seeing my print there every day, especially as I got older. It felt like leaving a legacy for the younger kids.

After school, we would go to the park, eat snacks, and do homework. We had some free time to unwind and run around. When we returned to her house, we all sat at the kids' tables with small chairs to read or get homework done. We had to be quiet, and she would check over our work to make sure we were on track. Afterward, we played games in the backyard and kicked around the soccer ball.

Sometimes we would play dress up, but one time—I don't recall how it happened—I got to dance my heart out.

One afternoon, most of the kids had been picked up. Roy, another camp attendee, and I cleared the floor of toys, rolled up the rugs, and pushed everything else in the big playroom to the side. We turned on music from the nearby tape player. As the sun set, the rays glowed through the windows.

Roy and I were just going for it—flailing around, hair loose, and sweat beading. No one else was around us, and it felt like we were the only two people in the world. I got so caught up in the music and being fully in my body that nothing else existed beyond that moment. Roy, a husky kid, had on jeans. He slid on the floor on his knees in a big encore move, out of breath, sweat dripping down the side of his little round face.

I looked over at him, and his eyes almost looked possessed. We lost track of time and moved our bodies until we couldn't anymore. It could've been five minutes or a full hour; I have no idea. I only remember the light fading, our breathing getting heavier, and our eyes locking from time to time. We mostly stayed in our own little orbits.

I wasn't thinking about what I was doing. I was just *being*. This was my first true moment of conscious embodiment. I got lost in the experience of moving. I was eight years old, tall for my age, and skinny. I hadn't yet learned to be self-conscious.

I moved uninhibited. Reflecting back now, I would definitely call this a sacred experience. Tapping into the true meaning of emotion—energy in motion. We were pure, limitless pulsing energy—joy, anger, fear, trust, and consciousness.

This pivotal experience vividly stuck with me. I don't know where that kid is now, but I wonder if it impacted him the same way. This was a defining point in how I related to moving my body. The key was the *combination* of energy and movement. It wasn't one or the other but rather the integration of both.

Just energy cycling around can be ungrounding and uncontained. That's when we get flighty spiritual people who don't have a firm grasp on reality. But on the other end, solely physical movement without awareness of the energy is just exercise or repeating steps. When you watch someone on stage, this can be the difference between someone being a "good dancer" and having that thing you can't look away from. Often, in a music video within a group of dancers, there's usually someone who stands out, who's got that extra *oomph*. They have an X factor you can't quite define or put your finger on, but you feel it. It draws you in.

Since then, I've had the pleasure of working with some of the most incredible dance teachers in the world. From twelve to seventeen, our preprofessional dance company would go to NYC for summer dance intensives. We had a special *in* that allowed us to attend a program typically for college kids and professional dancers over eighteen. One of the dancers from our company grew up to be a part of this illustrious company in New York. That dancer actually came full circle back to Atlanta and taught at my high school years later.

Getting to dance with professionals at this level was a supreme privilege. There was a huge age gap between us and the rest of the attendees. We were called "the kids," and every summer, this was the highlight of my year. From a very young age, I idolized dancers and would fangirl over the company members and teachers. They were all incredible. This specific dance company is not only one of the best in the world, it is also intergenerational and taught me about the possibility of dancing into your fifties and beyond.

This was rare, as there's a stereotype that a modern dancer's career is over at thirty—or twenty-six, depending on who you ask. For ballet dancers, it's even earlier. But this company had people who were in the company for over twenty years. The elders were revered, not pushed out. It was such an inspiring experience to be surrounded by celebrity dancers and mentors who were within reach.

During the intensives, we typically danced eight hours a day for three weeks. We attended rehearsals and performances, and every once in a while, we got to have some one-on-one time with a member of the company. They were like rock stars! At the end of every dance intensive, I asked each company member to write me a short note or sign their name in a notebook. I was a sentimental kid. I always wanted something to hold on to from the summers. I still have these and look at them from time to time to see the advice, stories, and wisdom they passed on to a younger version of me.

Our two companies ran parallel to each other, and we watched one another grow up. We saw some members start as apprentices and then move into junior roles, and ultimately become full-blown company members. They also saw us grow—literally, getting taller, bodies changing, hitting puberty, and going through that awkward tween to teenage stage. I had a crush on one of the male dancers, as most of us did. Of course, there was about a twenty-five-year age gap, but that didn't stop me from imagining our life together in some alternative reality.

After my fourth summer with the company, I had taken most of the classes offered and particularly enjoyed choreography and composition. During the year back home, we focused a lot on contact improvisation: practicing giving and sharing weight, moving with other bodies in space, and exploring responding to one another in the moment. We followed different exercises and learned to safely connect, lift, move one another, and track the empty space between the group. Now I look back at this and see the powerful energetic connection that runs through dance companies. You have to be very aware of the space, the group as a whole, and how each person contributes.

Every summer, our dance director told us to pick a mentor, and to watch how they moved, learn from them, and see if they would watch and give us any feedback in return. It was incredibly special to connect with one of these rock star dancers one on one for even five minutes. After years of having a long-term crush on Saulo, I asked if he wanted to move together after class one day. He said, "Yes, and we can work on sharing weight."

I had a lot of self-consciousness around my body at that point, and this invitation was a very big deal. I was the tallest person in our company, and my body had started to change in unexpected ways. Over the previous few years, my body sprouted curves, a belly, and breasts, which was not exactly celebrated in dance at that time. I was always praised for losing weight and often cast as "the boy" due to my height.

I didn't get chosen to partner a lot, let alone be lifted. The idea of leaning into someone who was bigger and stronger than me was exciting.

I met Saulo in the studio, and we warmed up a bit. Then I followed him through a few exercises. He asked me to lean into him and share my weight. It was tough for me to let go. I hadn't been dropped, exactly, but had definitely had partners comment about my weight, which didn't feel very good as a teenage girl going through puberty. The best way for me to relax and go with the flow was to close my eyes. So I took a breath and shut my eyes.

Saulo placed his hand on my back—specifically between my scapula—and said, "Breathe in and out of this space." He was pointing to just behind my heart, where I felt the light pressure and heat from his hand. I focused on expanding my breath into my back and letting him guide me.

We did a bit of a "follow the leader" and an exercise about listening to the point of contact, but it felt hard for me to fully trust. Of course, it was only partly about trusting a partner. The bigger piece was about trusting myself and being kind with the thoughts in my head.

We started with our hands, as they're the easiest point of connection—touching hands like in a high five motion and pushing into each other, giving resistance, playing with giving more or less weight until we each felt comfortable leaning in with more weight. I've used this exercise many times since then. After working with hands as the main point of contact, we graduated to a more advanced level without hands, using our backs, necks, legs, shoulders, feet, and more to initiate sharing weight.

I kept my eyes closed to try and follow better—to get out of my head. I had a tough time and was so nervous with that flitty energy in my stomach. I didn't want to give up but also wasn't fully trusting yet either. I knew when I truly move with someone, there's a part of us that can merge. It's more than physical and involves energetically touching and connecting as well.

It can be really intimate and beautiful.

After he led me around the room, leaning into each other and playing with sharing weight a bit, he asked me to guide him. He then closed his eyes. I stood there a little awkward and awestruck. I got quiet and focused on my breathing. I reached out for his arm to start. I tilted him off his center to travel across the floor. We leaned into each other back to back, rolling off one another, and I began to feel energetically altered, shifting into that soft focus, paying attention to the peripheral and space between. I reconnected to that feeling on the wooden floor after school when I was eight.

Nothing else mattered. No one existed but the two of us. But it wasn't the two of us as people. We transformed into more than that. We were actual *energy in motion*, merging to make a third thing, radiating love and courage into the world.

It felt like the lifeblood of the universe ran through our veins, and we were simply vessels. It verged on channeled dancing: Spirit moving through, around, and between us. It was beautiful. Again, it could've lasted only a few minutes or hours. Time was irrelevant.

At the end, I placed him back on his feet, so he took back his full weight. I removed my hands from his arms and quietly let go after being so close.

He opened his eyes and blurted out, "I love you." It took my breath away. "I love this. Dancing like this was so fun!" he continued.

I exhaled. He didn't mean it in the way I thought at first. But I felt it. It was pure love—the kind that doesn't take human form or become anything beyond that moment.

It was magical to be perceived and held in this way—two people and Spirit creating together or tapping into something bigger than us. I'd call that love—a deep, effervescent, full love.

I left the studio buzzing and breathless.

This moment guided me toward exploring a more intentional embodied energy practice. The only piece missing was a reflective or processing piece. I really wanted to talk about it, to share and debrief with someone. But it felt too delicate and like anyone outside the experience wouldn't understand.

So I wrote about it. I journaled that night, cheeks turning slightly pink with exhilaration and joy, like I stumbled upon something nameless that only existed in that moment.

Embodied spirit? Maybe. There weren't quite words to describe it.

It was glorious though.

All I could think was, *This! More of this, please.*

16

Everyone Has Their Own Montana

There was a long-standing tradition at Guilford for first-year Bonner Scholars to travel to the Crow Reservation in Montana to support, learn from, and work for the community for ten days.

Each year, the Bonner program invited about twelve students to participate. Their mission is to support kids from lower-income families to help pay college tuition by participating in service-learning opportunities while at school. There is a deep commitment to critical thinking, anti-racism training, and learning about power and privilege and how we each individually fit into systems.

Throughout the year, we reflected on questions and critiques about "doing community service," especially as a white person—what it meant to serve and understand our impact. Most of the scholars in the program were students of color. The white students were the minority. The Bonner Scholar Program was the most impactful part of my college experience, and I loved both the intellectual exploration along with the real-world experience. It helped balance being in the "Guilford Bubble" as a college student.

I was excited for the big trip to the reservation at the end of freshman year because of my connection to Native American spirituality and teachings. One piece of exchange for our work was the opportunity to participate in traditional Crow ceremonies.

I was both most excited and nervous about this piece because, throughout my studies with the Lakota work, we had to *earn* the right to partake in ceremonies after years of training. The leaders of the program told us we would have at least one opportunity to attend a sweat lodge on the reservation. If we wanted to participate, we were welcome.

I talked to Mom about this before I left since it felt like "jumping steps" in my own training journey. My mom was several years ahead of me in working with the Lakota Teacher, and she had participated in a few sweats, but I hadn't been invited yet.

"If you feel ready while you're there, I think it's okay to go for it. It's a different tradition and different context. Keep an open heart and stay hydrated," Mom advised.

We slept on cots in teepees and could see the open sky peeking through at night. We worked during the day with the leaders of the tribe. During the entire trip, the group split down the middle by gender—the guys with the Medicine Man and the women with the Medicine Woman, each assigned "gender-appropriate" tasks. While this rubbed me the wrong way, I knew we were on their land and were there to learn, contribute, and follow their traditions.

As a woman, I was assigned the task of sorting, steaming, and organizing clothing in the tribal thrift store. Other women worked in the kitchen to help prepare meals and clean. The guys were sent out with the Medicine Man to chop wood, move heavy supplies, and help repair and build structures. At night, we all came together for dinner, and our group leader would facilitate a debrief of the day.

After spending several days on the reservation, working hard, and getting to know the Medicine Woman, I felt more at ease about participating in a sweat lodge. I shared with two of my close friends on the trip about how big a deal this invitation was. They attempted to understand but couldn't quite empathize. They thought it was going to be a cool experience as opposed to a step in the larger process I'd been studying and progressing in for years.

The sweat was powerful, and I got to participate in more than one that week. The Crow Medicine Woman was much more casual than my Teacher. It didn't feel like there were as many rules or specifications. All the students in the group were welcome to participate, no matter their faith background or skill level. It was more about a cultural exchange for most people than a right of passage.

At the end of the week, one of the Medicine Woman's children was going to graduate high school. This was a big deal because he had several medical conditions when he was young, and the doctors didn't think he would live that long. They had planned a big celebration, and the family wanted to honor this milestone by holding a peyote meeting.

As someone who has always felt nervous about experimenting with substances or plant medicine, this opportunity caught me off guard. I have never really been drawn to drugs, and hallucinogens didn't necessarily excite me as it did some other students. I knew we would be experiencing this within a ceremonial context, but I had to decide if I was ready.

The Medicine Man came and talked to the group. "This is a celebration, and we need your help. Men, you'll be helping to build the teepee from scratch, skinning the bark off the poles and setting up the large communal teepee. Women, you'll be cooking the meal to break the fast and nourish the group the next day. Everyone is invited to participate, but it's very important you deal with your fear before you step inside the circle. We'll be fasting for twenty-four hours, and we'll be working with the peyote medicine to guide us. Let me know if you have any questions."

I was stunned. Of course I had questions, but I couldn't formulate any at that moment. Were we all just going to jump into this? I didn't even have time to talk with Mom, but I left her probably the strangest voicemail of our lives.

"Hey, Mom, wanted to give you a heads up we've been invited to participate in a peyote meeting this weekend. It will be Saturday night through Sunday, and I'll try to call you after, but not sure how I'll be. Love you!"

I wanted to do it. It was an amazing opportunity to participate in a medicine ceremony and work with plant medicine in a respectful and held way.

Throughout the week, I'd been getting closer with different people in the group as we were paired up to complete certain tasks. One woman I'd seen from afar during the school year worked with the prison literacy group on campus, which I joined the next year as a volunteer and witnessed some of the most beautiful truth-telling I've ever seen in my life.

This other student was a little intimidating, played rugby, and looked like she could beat you up at any time. We'd never really crossed paths, but one day, we were paired together to drive and pick up some heavy bags of seeds to bring back to the reservation.

On the drive, we started talking about family. Adaego was first-generation Nigerian, and her family lived in the same city as our college. She grew up locally and was still pretty close to her family. I shared I had lesbian moms, was from Atlanta, and didn't know much about Greensboro, the city surrounding Guilford.

It got quiet for a minute in the truck, and then she said, "Yeah, I'm bi." I held my tongue because I felt like she was very much a lesbian but knew it wasn't my place to label someone else's sexuality. And maybe she didn't want to go there... We didn't really know each other, and her sharing her sexual orientation stirred some butterflies in my tummy. I didn't know why at the time.

I had gone through a major breakup in the spring. My boyfriend, Danny, had been my first love. We weren't together very long, but he was the first guy I ever said "I love you" to, and it was the first time I felt that whirlwind where there was no need to eat, sleep, or even breathe, living purely off adrenaline and love.

It felt like an inconvenience to have to go to class, just waiting to see each other again. He was the only thing on my mind for months, and all I could do was wait for his embrace and the opportunity to spend more time together.

Both the relationship and breakup consumed me. I'd been nursing a broken heart for a few months, mostly by not making eye contact with anyone we used to know as a couple, trying to connect with friends, eating enough food to sustain me, and dancing. Choreography had been an important part of my high school experience, so when I came to college, I continued that path.

I put all my feelings into dance and choreographed a piece that semester about love and heartbreak. During the end of year performance, my piece expressed waves of loss and the shakiness I felt trying to survive having and then losing my first love. The performance was hard but healing. Even though it had been a couple months, I still felt like I was walking in a gray cloud of sadness, and nothing really worked to snap me out of it.

Going into this peyote meeting, I knew I wanted to open my heart again. I didn't know exactly what to expect, but I felt ready for transformation. We entered the teepee with prayers and respect to honor Lela's son. A fire was at the center and an altar. The Medicine Man conducted the peyote meeting, called in all the directions, and invited the community in one by one.

I found it interesting that over 80 percent of the people present were men, yet they told us in the Crow tradition, a peyote meeting is not permitted to begin or be conducted until a woman is present. Lela entered the teepee last and sat in a reverential spot, having her represent the Divine Feminine energy for balance.

The trip to Montana really illuminated some pieces around gender for me that felt uncomfortable, to say the least. The Medicine Man spent time throughout the week with the male students, and he favored and took care of them differently than the women. It often felt like the female students were an afterthought. I did my best to let it go and focus on why I was there.

I wanted to lean into this ceremony and did a lot of work to keep my fear and nervousness in check and not bring it into the space. He started the ceremony by passing a hand-rolled paper of cedar and tobacco. We each smoked it, and that opened the space and started to interweave the energy of the group. Everything was done communally.

That was the first and only time tobacco has touched my lips, and I held it in the context of ceremony. Next, the peyote tea was passed around. We each took a sip, inviting the medicine into our systems. We were warned about the purging that the medicine could trigger, and the leaders laid down a firm guideline that if we got sick to stay in the teepee and not leave the space.

"Lean down and dig a little hole in front of you if you have to throw up. Then cover it with dirt and return to your seat." As the medicine took effect, I started to hear people getting sick around me. I held down the bitterness and looked directly into the fire in the center.

"Please, please," I silently prayed, "show me something to heal my heart."

We sat in two circles packed tightly together, one not even a foot in front of the other, around the central fire. People were on my left, right, and behind me. I liked having direct access to the fire, but I wasn't *seeing* anything. I'd heard of the hallucinations or visions people can have with peyote, and in the coming years, this served as a catalyst to study indigenous art inspired by plant ceremonies.

The peyote tea was passed around along with peyote buttons to consume. For a long time, I didn't really feel anything, and the flavor was super earthy and intense. It was tough to ingest, and since we didn't really know what we were doing, I cautiously took what was given to me until I felt intuitively like I had taken enough.

Sitting directly on the ground, hunched over my crossed legs, I tried to make small adjustments. This was the most physically uncomfortable I'd ever been in my life. The way we were seated so close together didn't leave room to stretch out or move around. We had to stay seated, especially since everyone was having their own experience and I didn't want to interrupt. While the community sang or the Medicine Man played the flute, I rocked slightly and tried to lean into the discomfort.

We were in the teepee for eighteen hours, staying up overnight, sleep deprived, cramped and listening. I prayed for something to come. Finally, I gave up on "seeing something" floating in the air like how I imagined hallucinogens work and closed my eyes.

A vision struck me of a fire in my heart reaching toward the fire at the center of the circle. The image evolved into a naked version of me, rising from my heart and walking out toward the fire. She moved in front of me, stepping on the Earth. I could see and feel her presence. She was tall with her arms waving slowly. But at the end of her arms and legs were flames.

She was made of fire.

I saw her approach the fire and melt into it, dancing and swaying as the flames engulfed her entire being. As she integrated into the flames, her body joined the logs and the Earth, getting smaller and going deeper underground. As she merged with the Earth, she suddenly rose back up through the fire—three, five, seven feet in the air, growing taller and taller as she danced back toward me—back into my body, merging with my skin.

I felt cleansed and whole for the first time in months. My heart had returned.

At that moment, Adaego touched my leg. I don't think there's any way she could've known what had just happened to me. It felt electric. My heart was whole again, and then this woman was beside me. I didn't know what to do, so I reached my hand over to pat her knee. We sat in silence, and I cried a few tears of relief, getting so much more than I went there for—ultimately coming back home to myself.

• • • • •

After many hours of sitting, the Medicine Woman rose and invited Adaego and me—the only two women students left in the ceremony—to follow her outside. I felt lucky both for the break and the special acknowledgment of our presence. We went outside to help Lela change clothes and get ready for the next phase of the ceremony. Sitting on the back of a truck, Lela dangled her legs over the edge as we fussed with her moccasins.

"Is this right?" I asked Lela as I kneeled on the Earth to tie her laces. It was around three a.m., pitch black, and cold outside the teepee, but I was grateful to move my body and get some fresh air. We'd been sitting scrunched together for hours.

I looked up at the sky and the darkness that surrounded us. I remember not being able to see anything distinct until I looked at the river nearby. It was glorious—a teal blue, almost neon in color, glowing in the night. The peyote had definitely taken effect, and I felt drawn to the movement of the water and started to zone out and marvel at its color.

"Help me, ladies! We have to get back inside. This is a quick change." We laughed as we did the best we could with all the little details of her regalia while being on a mind-altering substance. I'm sure it would've been quite comical to watch, but at the moment, I just remember trying to focus so hard on making my fine motor skills do what they were supposed to.

As the Medicine Woman's feet touched the Earth, we all successfully gathered ourselves and headed back into the teepee. It felt like it was a mile away, but I knew it was only a few feet—and logically tried to tell myself we had already accomplished this task before when we exited, so it had to be possible to return. The comic relief was welcomed through such an intense overnight experience. We all held hands reentering and repressing giggles.

Returning to our seats, I looked back into the fire—my guiding light, center, and way home.

• • • • •

Many hours later, as the first round of water was brought through the teepee door to break the fast, I saw the sun shine for the first time in what felt like forever. This seemed like the longest night I'd ever lived. Seeing the dawn come through the doorway was magnificent, but not as magnificent as having our first sip of water and the first bite of corn.

Together, we broke the fast, singing, praying, and honoring that we made it through the ceremony!

Smiles and tears broke out across the community. Congratulations were given to Lela's son, and when it was finally time to end the ceremony, we crawled through the door outside to be born again and greet the day.

"Brothers and sisters, welcome!" the Medicine Man greeted each of us as we emerged from the teepee. Turning to one another, we started hugging, openly crying, and celebrating. It felt like we had changed, both individually and communally—even if we didn't know exactly what happened. The energy felt fresh and revitalized.

I turned to Adaego and said, "Thank you, sister!" I didn't know at the time she actually scoffed a little as she hugged me and rolled her eyes behind my back as she was thinking, *Sister, my ass.* I was just reveling in having my heart returned to me.

Later, we joked about that moment.

She was the first woman I loved, and we dated for two years after that. It always felt special to me that our connection formed beside the fire ceremony, where my heart was cleared and I truly fell back in love with myself.

• • • • •

At the end of the week, we went to the airport and said our goodbyes. The group headed to board planes in twelve different directions, but before we split, a couple of close friends and I shared our experiences.

"I feel so excited and clear about my next move," Emma said. "I think I'm going to look into being an ESOL teacher for adults."

"That's awesome! What about you, Amy? What are you leaving with?"

"I actually don't think I'm coming back to Guilford next year. I'm super burned out and may need time off."

"Woah, that's a big decision. Keep us posted over the summer with what you decide."

"For sure. And what about you, Meg?"

"We definitely all had our own Montana. I mean, I'm leaving with my heart more intact and maybe being attracted to a woman. What do I even do with that information?" I asked exasperatedly. We had such different experiences, almost like we spent the last week in different universes.

From that point forward, Montana symbolized for me when a group of people are in the same place but having wildly different experiences. None of my other friends discovered they were potentially queer on that trip. As I hugged them goodbye and boarded the plane to Atlanta, I pulled out my journal and wrote, *I think I like Adaego, but I don't think I'm gay. What does that mean?*

This particular ceremony helped me step more into my most authentic self, and even though it took time to adjust and fully embrace it, I love that my first experience of my own queerness was in a sacred connection and ceremony.

17

Concentric Circles of Connection

I learned early in life to pay attention to my body. When I began taking dance classes, the strive for perfection and discipline seemed to take over. But it also gave me the gift of paying attention to form and movement in a profound way.

My favorite part of dance has always been when I stop thinking. There's a sweet spot between a class being so hard that I can't comprehend the combinations and have to keep moving just to survive, or other times where a class is too easy and my brain drifts off. But then there's the "Goldilocks moment" where it's just right, and I'm so engaged my body has taken over and I don't have to think about each step.

It took me years to trust my body knows what to do, even if it doesn't. This refers to an internal, innate sense of responsiveness rather than a cognitive sense of knowing.

Learning to lean into our natural instincts, trust our gut, and listen to the intuitive knowing within each of us can be frightening for some people. But it's also so liberating and ultimately what this all whittles down to.

Most people do not know how to listen to their body, let alone trust it. Essentially, it was conditioned out of us. The narrative we are taught is that logic and intellect rule the world. However, we are walking around with an incredible network of neurons, bones, skin, and muscles that *know things* beyond the purely logical brain.

We don't have to join a dance company to experience this. Of course, everyone is different. But here's the secret…

If you have a body, you have access to move beyond thinking and constantly pushing through life. Instead, the focus shifts to presence, taking up space, and connecting with something bigger than us simply by existing.

Often, this is not taught in mainstream culture.

One of my favorite modern dance exercises is to have a group walk around the room with the assignment to find the empty space. We play with the pacing and move faster and faster, leaping, jumping, rolling on the ground, moving quicker and quicker, brushing past people, hoping to pay such close attention you don't knock into each other's skulls. Of course, this has happened to me—more than once. But the goal is to find the empty space. This also feels just like Spirit.

It's learning to listen between the lines, paying attention to how we can graze humanity without bowling them over, learning how to get close but not too close, even syncing our breath without overstepping a boundary.

Connection is a big multilayered concept. My brain breaks it down into three concentric circles to represent the layers, beginning with the inner circle, or the connection to self. Then the middle layer represents connecting with the collective or whoever is present in the experience at the time. The outer layer represents the connection to energy. Sometimes the final layer refers to the global impact or our connection with Spirit—or something "bigger than us".

The final layer is often intangible. It's living, breathing, and evolving in response to the first and second layer as a collective of people connect and create something new.

When looking at these three layers, we start in the center with ourselves, focusing on connecting to the inner voice, higher wisdom, and simple knowing that comes from truly listening in.

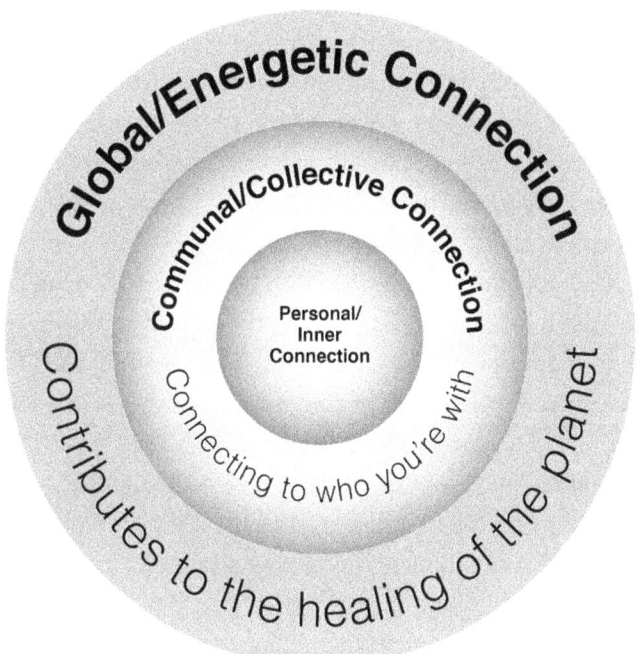

One pivotal moment for me in understanding that first layer occurred during a leadership retreat where we were doing high ropes courses as a group. I do not enjoy heights, and every single bit of the experience was hellish for me.

One of the other participants had the gall to tell me, "Look for the silver lining, like a flower peeking through the concrete."

I gave him a death stare. "Not the time for silver linings." My body shook for five minutes before even leaving the ground.

The task in front of us was to climb a very tall wooden pole alone. There were metal rungs dug into the side of it at various intervals, and you had to use both your upper and lower body strength to pull yourself up. Some people were pros and tackled both their physical and mental fears and scaled the pole with no problem. Others had different degrees of logistical success—getting a few feet off the ground, half way up, or even just on to the first rung. Each person had a different lesson to learn, and since this was a leadership retreat, those lessons were discussed, analyzed, journaled, and shared thoroughly.

The moment I was clipped into the harness, I began crying. With a helmet strapped tightly around my chin, my hair swept underneath, my body shaking, I approached the wooden pole. The focus of this workshop was on self-leadership, and for me, that meant developing more inner faith. I would rather have been up there with someone else, or collaborating on a larger task, but when it's solely me, I'm forced to face the most challenging competition I have: myself.

I started climbing the pole as my group stood firmly on the ground. The leader of our group shouted some motivating words, and others gave advice. "Look for the rung above your left foot." I kept focused on the singular task in front of me, one piece at a time, to try not to get too overwhelmed. I was still shaking but making progress.

"What are you moving toward?" Sofia, the group leader, yelled up to me.

"Nothing. Shhh. I don't want to be metaphorical." I kept my eyes right in front of me, clasping the metal rung until my hands turned white.

"Fine. You're almost there. Almost to the top. Keep going."

I reached up for the last foothold and yelled back, "Now what?"

I'd seen other people do it, but the next step seemed impossible. You had to hoist your entire body weight on top of the pole, with barely enough room for both feet. But there was nothing else to hold on to. Some flexible people sort of lunged their way up that last impossible step. Others who were strong muscled their way through, heaving one leg up and standing triumphantly at the top, basking in the glory of their work, arms spread wide, taking it all in.

"Trust your body," my friend yelled. "Trust your body," she said again.

I heard her. I loved that. It wasn't *trust yourself, trust your capabilities...* Instead, her words redirected me to *trust the body that got me up here.*

It settled for me conceptually. Physically, I was still a shaky, crying mess, but I heard her words in a way that was absolutely perfect. So, after many deep breaths and a couple tries, I knew my body was strong, flexible, and resilient enough from all my dance training.

I didn't know what to do, but my body did. So I let it lead me.

One hand on top of the pole, I launched a leg up in a fierce lunge and reached out in front of me, holding onto nothing. "Spirit, god, Spirit, oh god, Spirit, hold me!" I chattered as I shook. I leaned into my quad and willed my other leg up to meet me. One swift movement, from a deep plié to standing on top with two feet together. I felt the pole moving from my jitters, all the way down into the Earth.

I hardly had my eyes open. I was scared, trembling, and wanting it all to be over, barely cognizant of my leadership cohort cheering me on from the ground. I briefly looked down and gulped.

"Look around you! Take it all in. Look at where you are!" Sofia shouted.

"I don't know if I can…"

"You did it! Look up at the sky. Look what you reached toward. You've made it up there. You might as well enjoy it!"

With my helmet sliding a little over my eyes, I cautiously opened my hands down by my side in a receiving position and looked up.

"The sky cracked open literally at that moment. It was palpable. I could feel the energy shift. Damn, you're powerful," Sofia told me once I was back on the ground.

I saw it with my eyes. I looked into the nothingness and reached for Spirit, *here with me, around me always.* At that moment, all three layers were present. Trusting in myself and my body in the first layer of the concentric circles: connection with self. The second one, of the collective—the whole group cheering me on and willing me to keep going—and finally, the last circle, the impact of my experience reverberating outward. What we wove together that day was magic.

I felt the global and energetic impact ripple between my body and the sky.

In that moment, my entire being opened up, and waves radiated across the Earth.

That day, I understood on a cellular level a new layer of trusting myself, my body, and the impact I'm here to create.

The body is both a source of wisdom and a tool for integration.

The body is:
Source
Resource
Resourceful
Energy
Connection
Reconnection
Sacred
Holy
Divine
Spirit
In you
In me
Inside all of us
Surrounding us
Always

If you are a parent, imagine if your child knew deep down in the fabric of their being that *their* very own body came from Source—Creator energy—that their body can be sourced for wisdom, guidance, and information. *And* they can learn to trust themselves.

If you don't have kids, imagine if you could go back in time and pause the exact moment where you cut yourself off from trusting your gut knowing. Let's be real, there's probably more than one moment, as it happens millions of times throughout our lives, where we jump into our mental space and stay there—sometimes for just a breath, sometimes for years. Many people never come back down—to our truth, to our gut instinct and power, to our embodied wisdom that exists below the neck.

Imagine if you could *re*-source that road for yourself and for your child. We cannot protect anyone from experiencing the harsh realities of the world. Envision a life where you teach yourself or your kid how to re-route, just like on a GPS, and take the road back to themselves more often, more frequently than drifting from their source, from their truest self, leaving themselves in a world of self-doubt and dis-member-ment.

It is our job to *Re-member* who we are.

In shamanism, this is an ancient concept—the act of *Re-membering* our souls. Some call it soul retrieval; some see it as literally piecing back together parts of ourselves that split off. Any way you envision this, it is a mending process, a healing that must be done in community rather than individually.

When we work to heal ourselves, we amplify healing energy in general: collectively, within our own families, and across the planet. Each person's healing impacts both future and past generations. When there is a large societal wound, such as the disconnect between our body, mind, and spirit, we have to seek healing on a collective level.

It takes great courage to do this work both for ourselves and future generations. Remember, we must do our own work before asking others to join us.

18

Intuitive Work

I listen to my body when I'm working with clients. Messages from Spirit sometimes come through audibly, visually, or as a visceral sense of tension, warmth, or ping to pay attention. It's not my job to assign meaning to it but rather to just *feel* into the signal my body is giving me. Ultimately, my job is to listen to Spirit speak through me, around me, and within whoever I'm working with at the time. I often hear more than the words people use, as their heart, body, and energy are also speaking.

Picking up on those unspoken messages comes from a blend of training, studying shamanic energy healing, and an innate sensitivity to feeling things "light up" in my body. Almost like the game of *Operation*, which alerts you when you touch the sides, certain parts of my body will flag my brain to pay extra attention. When I first started working with clients, I thought it was too strange to mention. But throughout coach training, the leaders told us to focus on "intuition, not interpretation."

This simple phrase can be lifesaving, both as a clinician and as a client, giving yourself permission to feel things without automatically translating and assigning meaning.

Once, during a phone session with a client, my feet kept tingling. I heard a message from my body to "pay attention to your feet." Since I couldn't see my client through the phone,

I followed the urge and said, "Hey, I know this might sound strange, but what do your feet have to do with this issue with your coworker? My feet are buzzing, and they want me to draw attention to them. Does that mean anything to you?" I didn't know the context, nor did I try to interpret the initial sensation.

She said, "That's so weird for you to pick up on. I stare at my feet when I'm overwhelmed. I'm trying to stay present, but I just want to run away." This small snippet really unlocked the conversation, and we talked about a new way to draw attention to her feet. We did some grounding visualizations and helped her create a new association with looking down, a more empowering perspective to redirect her habit of withdrawal instead of speaking her needs.

The long, winding road to claiming my power and stepping into my gifts continues to evolve. For the past ten years, I've worked with clients who are seeking to carve their own path in the world. Most of my clients identify as women or are part of the LGBTQ+ community and are looking for support on a variety of topics, including job transitions, difficult family dynamics, important conversations, wanting a romantic partnership, or connecting more deeply with their intuition. I refuse to choose a niche.

Together, we look at everything through a spiritual or intuitive lens, and it can be hard to pin down exactly what I do. Most of what I do is respond to what shows up in the moment. But if I had to call it something, I would say I provide emotional and energetic support to people going through "transition and transformation."

I started coaching a year after Mom died. It's the first thing she didn't know about me, and it has been really challenging to start a business in the midst of grief. The rollercoaster of entrepreneurship is not for the faint of heart. As I felt called to embrace my spiritual gifts throughout Mom's death and dying process, I began to synthesize my background in leading sacred ceremonies, intuitive healing work, and movement with coaching and leadership skills.

It's funny to look back at my childhood self, who would never in a million years have picked this as a career path. I was often embarrassed by the many levels of oddness Mom brought into my life. But ultimately, all those pieces I resisted became my spiritual path, my livelihood, and a journey back to the truest parts of who I am.

I name this for anyone else who feels lost or like they're swimming in the general territory of their gifts but can't name them yet. I worked on so many "elevator pitches" and filled out worksheets scratching out one word in exchange for another over and over again. It drove me crazy, until at a leadership training course, one of the leaders stated her purpose as "I create magic in every room I enter."

What? That's an option?

It sent tingles down my spine. The core of my work is creating space for others to fully embody and embrace who they are. I'm here to help people own their weirdness, reintegrate the pieces of themselves they may have discarded or shied away from, and come home to themselves. This may sound amorphous or vague, but it also makes space for a lot of truth.

In many ways, I picked up the baton of Mom's work and have carried forward her legacy. I didn't originally mean to, but when she was sick, I knew I couldn't waste more time doing something that wasn't right for me. I knew in order to survive after she passed, I would need to find my own thing.

One caveat: I would not become a therapist. My mom, biological father, godmother, and uncle are all therapists. So of course, instead of therapy, I chose coaching—not a very far leap, but it uses many of the same skills of empathy, intuition, deep listening, and connecting. One of the biggest differences is I knew I wasn't in a space to focus on past trauma.

People ask me all the time, "How did you even get into this work? I've never heard of a Spiritual Coach before."

I share about my certification and training to sound official, and then I talk about my spiritual path and studying from such a young age. The coaching field has allowed me to integrate every part of who I am into how I support my clients: drawing from my leadership development courses, experiential training, and twenty-five-plus years of studying shamanism, energy healing, and embodiment practices.

> *When I was younger, Mom would tell me, "The goal is to just keep creating a better and better synthesis of the work you do."*

I saw a living example of this when Mom moved from being a therapist to utilizing reiki and energy healing as part of her sessions with some clients, when requested. That continued to transform as she stepped into her calling as a Spiritual Teacher. I saw her shift to having both clients and students. It inspired me behind the scenes as I watched her work evolve as she did.

Since beginning to work with clients, I've had people come to me from various backgrounds, from nurses, lawyers, parents, tarot readers, photographers, CEOs, or leaders looking to do life "a little differently." I help people lean into their intuitive gifts and realign with their inner wisdom.

I've noticed a theme with my clients over the years that no matter what they do for work, they are often secret healers, sometimes holding that private even from themselves.

Many of my clients never fully developed their spiritual gifts as a child, and now, as adults, they aren't sure how to integrate those gifts into the rest of their lives. It can be disorienting, especially if you grew up in a family that wasn't supportive of this type of inner exploration.

As a Spiritual Guide, I lead people inward to develop a stronger relationship with themselves, their soul, and their calling. This transformational work ultimately came from my original wounding, which is quite common in the healing profession—to pull purpose from the parts of ourselves or pieces of our lives not honored.

As a kid, I longed to be normal and accepted, but when I realized I didn't have a shot at normalcy this lifetime, I shifted to creating opportunities for others to take up space as their true selves. Counterintuitively, finding acceptance wouldn't come from conforming to society's norms. It actually comes from leaning deeper into the "woo world" and stepping further into my power as a healer.

My guides have asked me to lean even further into the mystical realm and trust Spirit—which is not always an easy task when there's no roadmap. I get nervous of crossing the line between "acceptable weirdness" and being too out there to exist within the regular confines of society. For years, I've clung to city life to stay connected with friends and have access to all the city has to offer. But often, the messages I receive from my guides can be so out there I shush it away, hoping for a more reasonable option.

"No one will want that offering," I quip back, or I ask bluntly, "How would I even do that?" when my guides keep nudging me toward certain ideas or teachings. Unfortunately, my guides do not care about practicality or things like bills, money, or deadlines. They focus on the big energy they're here to move through me.

"Take people to the Earth to connect and talk to trees," they tell me.

"Oh, for sure. No further guidance needed," I respond sarcastically.

I've searched for years to find middle ground between the two worlds. Branding coaches have often asked me to use more practical words like "communication classes" instead of "sacred relationship workshops." It always felt like a pull between my soul and mainstream culture.

Some well-meaning mentors have told me to study neuroscience or get a more "legitimate" degree in organizational development to back up my intuitive knowing. I get it. Often, they come from a generation when you wouldn't be taken seriously without a certain degree or credentials. But I've lived outside the norm practically since birth.

After some back and forth and looking into more mainstream options, I decided I didn't want to get a master's degree just because it would look good on paper. The truth is there is no shamanic grad school that will prove my knowledge and depth of experience. No certification or piece of paper proves someone is *worthy* of doing this work.

There are trainings, of course, and while it is important to me to receive my spiritual teachers' blessing, I also recognize this *calling* cannot be credentialed.

It is a life path.

My intuition does not need a stamp of approval. It took me a long time to learn that.

In 2018, during a session with an intuitive reader, she told me, "Your life purpose is to be a successful Spiritual Teacher."

"Whew! That's not a small one," I said, making a face and clenching my teeth together to hold back my judgment.

I hadn't used those words for myself before. But after years of work, I can feel when something settles as truth in my body pretty quickly, and this one hit like an arrow directly through a bullseye.

Spirit helps me feel connected, held, and supported. It's always felt like where I most belong. I joke I began searching for my life purpose at the age of eight. Life often feels like an unending quest.

Once I'd worked through some of my feelings, I knew truly embracing a transformative career path would allow me to keep a foot in both worlds, grounding into the reality of supporting people instead of solely hanging out with the stars, where I'm much more comfortable. As I put words to my energetic embodied experiences, I also give myself grace, knowing words can only capture so much of the ephemeral.

When I tune in to hear people's souls talking, I also get the honor of connecting with their sacred team.

Some people think of a sacred team like the characters from *Inside Out*—great movie! Other people call it their "inner boardroom" when I work with executives. I call it a "Council of Elders" that represents the wise parts of ourselves who see far beyond the present moment problem and can offer us guidance. They chime in and share their wisdom when called on.

Once, when working with a client who was navigating some difficult family dynamics, we called on the members of her Inner Council, and her dog, who died years before, showed up to support her.

There are no strict rules for who can be part of your Inner Council.

For this client, the dog represented unconditional love and always looking for the good in people. Trying on that perspective actually shifted how she viewed the entire situation. She moved from stuck and angry to compassionate and available to hear what her family had to teach her in that moment. She stayed open to shifting beyond the "I'm right and they're wrong" stance.

Some people feel like they can't access those inner voices of wisdom, and many people feel cut off from their intuition entirely, especially if something traumatic happened and they feel like they can't trust themselves anymore.

For instance, I had another client who found out her partner cheated on her for years, and the lies came to the surface. She was in shock. They broke up, and when she started to explore dating again, she felt like she couldn't trust herself.

She told me, "If all those signs were there and I just didn't see them, how could I possibly trust anybody? I'll just keep looking for red flags and be on edge." I threw out the idea that her healing wasn't about learning to trust a new person—but was ultimately about learning to trust herself again. She cried tears of recognition and acknowledged the fear she was holding.

She wanted to get better at listening to herself and taking action based on what she heard. Intuitive healing is an active, living process. It's not a one-and-done.

We talked through her past relationship, and she started to identify the moments of *self-betrayal*—not when her partner betrayed her, but when she didn't listen to her own *knowing*.

She could feel it in her body when we targeted those moments, like she had been struck. She's a powerful, smart woman who momentarily gave up her authority and trusted someone else above herself. She hadn't listened to friends when they pointed out some strange reactions or situations in her prior relationship. And ultimately, she didn't give herself credit for knowing that something didn't feel right.

Years ago, I heard a comedian refer to that thing we feel inside as god or Spirit or the Universe tapping us on the shoulder to get our attention. So every time you hear yourself say—either internally or externally—"something doesn't feel right here," that *something* is the Divine knocking on your door. I'd also call that *something* as *intuition*. They are interchangeable.

Spirit speaks to us through our intuition.

As a small example, early in 2020, I wanted to go on a hike with my dog. I'd taken this hike several times over the last few years, but this particular day, I had a hard time leaving the house, and I didn't understand why. I thought it might be anxiety due to the unknowns with COVID-19 (pre-vaccine). It took me several hours, but I finally left the house.

After the thirty-five-minute drive, I found the turnoff to the trailhead blocked by police. They shut down the entry on a Saturday—odd. As I made the U-turn out of there and pulled over to choose a new destination, I felt bummed to have wasted time.

I heard this whisper in my mind: "That's why you couldn't leave the house on time. We were trying to stop you from making the drive." My guides often chime in, that Inner Council I mentioned, with short simple sentences. It annoyed me to not be able to go where I planned, but I also reflected on the moment at home where I thought, *Well, this is weird. I'm having a really tough time leaving the house.* But I pushed beyond it and went anyway.

That moment—my decision to ignore the message and push through—was a tiny yet important one of self-abandonment. Those moments add up and can be as small as considering directions or as major as knowing something is up in a relationship and ignoring it, or sensing it's time to leave your job but choosing to stay anyway.

Learning to catch that internal moment is the key to creating self-trust.

It's similar to building trust in relationships with others, where every time someone says, "I'll see you there," and then they actually show up, that builds trust. If they flake at the last minute, it can weaken the bond you're building because you feel like you can't count on them.

Now, consider that same scenario with yourself: Every time you say, "Yes, I'll go on that walk today," and you do it, you strengthen the connection to that inner trust and power. Or when you meet someone and immediately don't like their vibe but you decide to hangout anyway, and then it goes poorly. If only you had just listened to that part of you that *knew*. It's not to blame or beat yourself up. It's to redirect to that moment of knowing and to pause, recognize, and act on it over and over again when it comes up.

This builds a neural pathway of trust. We want to strengthen and deepen that groove in our system—whole body, mind, and spirit. One of my past clients calls me a "personal trainer for the soul," helping people build their intuitive muscles and creating a life filled with self-love and self-trust.

I worked with a client on learning to listen to herself again. When we hit a point where she could feel it in her body, I saw the shift. Emotionally, energetically, and intuitively, she was aligned. So happy, I exclaimed, "I see you—there you are! I can feel it coming together. You're nailing trusting yourself for maybe the first time in a long time."

She stopped me, with tears in her eyes, and said, "Or for the first time ever." This is the most powerful outcome I could hope for my clients—to love and trust themselves more. It changes *everything*!

Because when we truly listen and don't skip over the inklings, nudges, and whispers, it creates a powerful process of *coming home to yourself.*

It's meeting yourself at the door with open arms, welcoming you back from a very long trip of betrayal and longing for things to be different when really we needed an internal adjustment. I envision making space to truly listen, like pulling up a chair with a cozy blanket and a warm cup of tea. It's an invitation to be real with yourself and honor what comes up—fully and completely. There's no need to deny what you feel. This is a landing spot where you can take off your shoes and sit with your most trusted advisor, your inner wisdom and guidance.

It gives me chills to imagine you doing this.

I had another client come to me because she wanted to explore her fear of death. She was forty-two, in good health, and was about to be an empty nester. As we broached this big topic, I asked, "What are you truly looking for today during our session?" She broke down and simply said, "I don't feel like I have anyone to talk to about the deep stuff. I feel lonely and have a lot of questions. I'm not sure what I believe, but I think I'm scared of dying because I don't know what comes next."

I took a deep breath, and with a small smile on my face, I said, "No one knows for sure what happens when we leave this planet and body behind. But I'm happy to help you connect with Spirit *now* while you're alive so you can ask all the questions you want—and we will sit together and see what we hear." Her shoulders relaxed a bit, and she took a breath. "That sounds good."

She just didn't want to continue holding her fears alone.

In order to make space for her to connect with Spirit, I knew I needed to ground and open a channel—much like tuning into a specific radio station. At this point, my antenna to Spirit fully extended out toward the sky and down toward the Earth.

This is how I listen to messages from my intuition. I often start sessions by asking people to envision light from their heart reaching down into the soil beneath them, inviting Mother Earth to come support us and join us on this call, and then invite the energy to rise up in our bodies and settle in our hearts, to feel the earth's solid ground below us.

With another deep breath, we extend that light from the heart up to Father Sky, reaching into the realm of all possibilities.

When we feel a powerful sense of expansion, we call the energy back down through the top of our heads and feel it meet in the center of the heart to create balance with the Earth energy and to feel embraced from above and below and hold space for the healing that needs to take place.

I call in guides, allies, and beings who love this client, and I stay open to who shows up. What I mean by that is, often, someone important will come join us from the client's Inner Council. I'm not a Medium specifically, though sometimes people who have passed on do show up in sessions. I'm very comfortable navigating grief, death, and dying, so sometimes clients open more to connecting with someone who has passed, even if it's new for them.

In one case, a client's Council member was actually another version of her instead of another person. It was her Future Self. Tapping into your Future Self is an exercise that involves visualizing a specific amount of time into the future—five years, fifty years, end of life, and so on—to zoom out and look back at this moment. This helps gain a greater perspective and ask for some soul guidance.

For this client, all of this was very unusual, but she was totally game to explore, even if she didn't know what she was getting into. It's my job to hold the space, create a sacred container for healing work to occur, and lead a debrief to help clients integrate after the session. A big reason I take an embodied approach is to deepen the wisdom and help people connect to a felt sense of their intuition and higher guidance. Feeling it in your body makes all the difference, as it's clear it's not a made-up idea or ethereal concept. It's something you can feel within your own skin.

In order to anchor this wisdom, I asked my client to have her Future Self give her an embodied practice she could do to tap into this energy after the session. This powerful being of love gave her simple directions to rub her thumb and first finger together down by her thigh to be able to call up her Future Self. It's a small gesture she could do at work or expand on in a more private space. This was a total surprise and one of my favorite aspects of this work. Together, we enter sacred space in collaboration and see what shows up between *you, me, and Spirit.*

I love connecting with something bigger than us, listening deeply to my own body, and tapping into the energy and essence of a client. In these spaces, I get to show up as my best self. All of my human challenges with my personal neurosis, anxiety, and general overthinking gets out of the way, and our souls meet up in a divine playground. I love thinking of sacred space in this way.

There will always be more to learn and transform. My ideal clients and I are both lifelong learners and will probably be seeking personal growth the rest of our lives. Supporting people through transformation, integration, and connecting deeply with their soul, inner wisdom, and unique gifts brings me great joy!

And, as wonderful as this sounds, each session isn't always wrapped up with a nice bow and a Hollywood ending. In coaching, they often say, "The work happens between the sessions." I would echo that and add that sometimes, when we enter an energetic or ceremonial space, the work is also happening during the experience. Energy is moving, beliefs are shifting, and our bodies are recalibrating to a sense of being held and supported. This can take a while to settle in, and I see our work together as an opportunity to walk beside each other for a time.

19

Finding My Place in Two Worlds

Mom taught me about finding my "power place," a physical spot on the Earth where we feel more connected to Spirit and can go to recharge. As a kid, I felt drawn to a very special place on Dreaming Bear's land. It had a small waterfall that pooled below, ran over moss-covered rocks, and led down into the river.

I would take crystals, stones, and stories to this place where the water met the land, the sun shining through the trees and warming my skin. At first, I would go there with Mom, and as I grew older, I started going on my own. One time, I saw a salamander and was entranced by its pink skin and quick movements. I loved that it could thrive both in the water and on the land. It felt magical to witness its ability to transition between the two and enjoy both.

This little waterfall was my special spot. The problem? I didn't know other kids my age who had "special earth spots," where they went to think, listen, and tap into something bigger; to watch the natural world evolve with awe and bring back messages and metaphors. I often felt out of place, like I couldn't quite bring my sacred work into my daily life, yet my daily life felt too loud to make space for the quiet reflection I craved.

So I learned to keep them separate.

Living in the in-between often leaves a person feeling as though they belong everywhere and nowhere at once. Because of this, bilingual or multicultural individuals often become bridge builders or translators for the people on either side. They adapt to constantly navigating both sides without necessarily having an identity that is fully seen and embraced by either.

This is when we feel like we aren't enough of either one but have shifted into an amalgamation of the two: an emergent third identity that embraces parts of both sides without having to choose one over the other.

We have to adapt to the differences and transform to thrive in both landscapes.

I fought this in-between identity for a while but have come to understand myself as a spiritual translator charged with bringing messages between the energetic and physical realms.

Living in two worlds, I often feel like an amphibian, moving between the human and spiritual domains. I slowly learned to take down the walls I'd created and started integrating Spirit into my daily life, intentionally making space to tap into my intuition and creating ways to connect that don't involve traveling up a mountain every time!

The language of Spirit is fluid, emergent, and shifting in real time. Spiritual translation work can feel like learning to breathe underwater.

I never really related to the butterfly as the emblem for transformation. While the journey of going into the cocoon and becoming goo, and then coming out in a whole new form is beautiful, it just doesn't feel like my story. I much prefer adapting, adjusting to the environment and creating a home both on land and in water.

According to the website Vocabulary.com, "the word *amphibian* comes from the Greek word *amphibios*, which means 'to live a double life.' The noun *amphibian* has its roots in the words *amphi*, meaning 'of both kinds,' and *bios*, meaning 'life.' The word is used for the class of animals that spend part of their lives in water and part on land" (vocabulary.com n.d.).

Maneuvering between land and water reminds me of the adaptation necessary to live in the mainstream world as a spiritual person. Sometimes the languages don't match up, or our original form—like the tadpole's tail—isn't what we need in the second part of our lives.

This metaphor contains many pieces: The origins of who we are from birth transform but remain within us as we adapt and change; or the pieces of ourselves we needed in the beginning no longer support our needs as we grow; and lastly, we embark in generational evolution of shedding and reclaiming certain traits we inherited from our parents we want to hold onto.

This reabsorption process reminds me of the innate sparks we feel during childhood, like when we get so curious about a topic we can't leave it alone, or have that one core memory that shapes the rest of our lives. For me, that was my performer self.

As a child, I did gymnastics, took piano lessons, asked for help recording songs and stories, and can't even imagine the number of times Mom heard me say "Watch me! Watch me, Mommy. Look, look at what I can do," then proceeded to do the same cartwheel over and over again until I got too dizzy to stand, insisting I could do it better.

"Are you watching?" definitely feels like a theme in my life. I look back at all the ways little Meg was creative—often not very good at something—but did it anyway. I was fascinated with drawing horses for a time and wrote an endless number of poems. I remember feeling like words poured out of me, and if I didn't write them down, I might die. The level of conviction and high drama was unmatched.

That thread, though—the part of me that wanted to be seen, have an audience, and perform—grew from a tiny seedling saying "watch me" to putting on an evening length show of my choreography at seventeen. The times I've honored my inner performer often led to a deep satisfaction and feeling of putting out meaningful work. However, as I've gotten older, sometimes the performer part of me lies dormant and feels like it burns down to embers. It's still there, the flame barely visible from the outside, but I feel a small rumble from within, like it's waiting to be reignited.

To other bridge builders and multilingual interpreters:

You are not alone. Whether you feel like a salamander, toad, frog, or newt, you are an incredible specimen existing in and between two worlds, adapting and changing to meet the environment—often existing in a third space that most people can't comprehend.

It's taken a really long time for me to find other "underwater breathers" or spiritual amphibians who exist between both worlds. It can be really lonely unless you find others who know how to speak both languages and don't need an explanation to understand who you are.

During one of the coach training weekends in Atlanta, I heard an intuitive message come through. I was feeling a little stuck in my head and out of place. At the end of the day, I went up to one of the leaders and shared this image of amphibious underwater breathers as a symbol for spiritual people navigating both worlds but always feeling like an outlier.

The next day, this leader put a little sticker of a fish on her name tag—a subtle nod to also identifying as someone who could breathe underwater and speak to Spirit.

I felt so seen and aligned. Even though fish aren't *exactly* the same, some do come to the surface seeking nourishment, almost like a spiritually curious person making contact with the other world from time to time. We were swimming in the same water, and that visual reminder made me feel like I found one of my people.

Anyone else feel like an underwater breather? Shifting, adapting, and evolving to move between one world and the other? You are courageous and have tremendous capacity to live within and between two worlds.

PART 3

20

Light Lifting Ceremony

"This is what you're meant to do," I heard my Spirit Guides whisper. "Lead people in ceremony."

I stood with open palms at the top of my mom's hospital bed with three other women gathered around. They listened intently as I led them through a light lifting ceremony. The purpose is to unwind the energetic anchor points to help someone release and detach from their physical body.

I've actually experienced this ceremony from the receiving side as well, covered in a sheet, eyes closed, lying on a massage table in the living room when Mom was still well. She and some of the other students needed a practice client, and I volunteered. The focus is on lifting the energetic body and clearing any attachments. Sometimes I could feel it, almost like someone tugging or pulling on certain energy centers—similar to chakras—and other times, I wanted clear proof of what was happening. As I lay with my eyes closed that day, I was listening to my body and trying to feel into what was actually loosening and detaching from my physical form.

Now the roles were reversed, and I was leading. I talked through the process slowly, and we raised our arms together to lift up her energy. I remember distinctly in this moment looking at these women and recognizing what was happening. At the absolute worst moment of my life, I was stepping into my spiritual gifts.

• • • • •

A few days later, Mom would leave her physical form and become completely Spirit. But in those last few days, she was having trouble leaving. It's like she was holding on. Day by day, we, as her care team, were barely making it through, sleep deprived and trying to surrender to the process. But when you're watching the person you love most in the world slowly slip further and further away, it's painful and harrowing.

Her body lay in that hospital bed, hooked up to 'round the clock pain meds. She was so warm but content—no longer responsive as the nurses turned her over to take her vitals. We had transitioned to a hospice facility a few days earlier. It was excruciating to acknowledge death in this way. It wasn't even "at our doorstep." We had actually approached it and moved in.

I didn't fear death or letting go. It was clearly time, but it seemed to go on and on.

Jokingly, I would talk out loud to Mom. "Okay, I put a candle by the window, you can go now. Mom, I blew it out and opened the door. You can go now. I'm going home to nap, you can leave too." Opening the door, closing it, saying goodbye, going for a walk, staying in the bubble, leaving the bubble—all the things the hospice nurses advised us to do.

Sometimes people let go when their loved ones are in the same room, waiting for them to settle and be present. Other times, people leave when someone leaves the room, and they seem to quietly escort themselves out with their last breath. She was stubborn.

Finally, we called in a really special hospice volunteer who was an "Intuitive." I had never heard that term before, but it foreshadowed my next steps on this path. She served as an amazing death doula and transitional mentor. She sat in the room with us and put on headphones, closed her eyes, and went on a journey. That's how she explained it.

After about fifteen minutes, she asked if we wanted to hear about what was happening for Mom. "Of course!" I exclaimed, with nervous short breaths anticipating what we would hear. Any information was helpful to know about why Mom was holding on when her body was shutting down.

The Intuitive told us, "Your mother is the most peaceful person I've ever met in this transition, and I've sat with a lot of people. I saw her by a river with her arms outstretched, waiting for someone who passed on before her, maybe her mom or grandmother, to welcome her to the other side. But as they approach, she's watching all the people she loved take care of her, as she took care of them. She gave a lot this lifetime and is practicing receiving. That's why she's still here. She's learning to receive love."

The Intuitive described it as Mom's spirit floating above us, watching us all move around her body as she looked down from the ceiling.

Tears ran down my face as I leaned forward in those pink pleather chairs. Mom cast a wide net of love, as evidenced by all the people who joined us in her care, but this image of her learning to receive hurt my heart. I wanted her to know it was okay to go. It was time, but death cannot be rushed. For the umpteenth time during this process, I felt powerless.

Unfortunately, powerless was my predominant experience and had been for many months.

I said all I needed to say, both long and short goodbyes. I had no regrets in how we spent our time, but I really leaned into the deep love and emotional connection we had together.

So much was left undone, especially knowing I'd be walking back into a life that no longer fit.

Nothing would be the same anymore.

I remember going to a coffee shop the week Mom died. I gave myself a pep talk beforehand. "Don't cry at the barista. Don't cry at the barista. Maybe never come back to this shop because you and your mom would come here. But definitely don't cry at the counter."

I barely made it through. Mom and I did everything together. And it was as though the world changed color—for most of my life, it had been green, and suddenly, everything was purple. It's not better or worse now that it's purple. It's just different. It feels impossible to do green things in a purple world.

People who didn't understand that the world changes colors, they don't tell you—of all those people you love, only a few will make it. It's like jumping off a ship and landing in a lifeboat, and instead of the five hundred people on board the big ship, you'll be heading into this next part of your life with only three of them, and they might not be the three you think. The folks you knew in your heart would be there when the worst of it went down are not the people who showed up. And the people you had zero expectations really come through for you during that time. It's wild and very counterintuitive, surprising, and painful.

These days, my grief community, or "sad friends" as one of the members calls us, is amazing. We're all part of a club no one wants to be a part of.

But the powerful thing is that it's the most important crew I've ever had.

This group of strangers who understand what it's like to lose *your* person.

My best friend in Atlanta and I became friends through dance class, and both our moms died within a year of each other. We still make inappropriate dead mom jokes, and I don't know what I would've done without someone who understood the impossibility of caretaking and then picking up your life and moving forward and moving on and surviving for the foreseeable future.

If you don't laugh at this next piece, it's probably because you haven't gone through unspeakable loss. And for anyone who does laugh, I'm sorry. I love you. You get it.

A few months after both of our parents passed, my friend and I stood in line for coffee and made a joke that we needed buttons on our shirts that said "My mom died. Get out of my way." This can topple into almost any area you need it to. "My mom died. Yes, I'd like free dessert." "My parent died—please bill this expensive dinner to her tab, but she's dead. So she won't be paying. Thank you for understanding." "Traffic? What is this? My mom is dead. Where are you all going with living parents?" This makes me snicker.

But dark comedy for dark times is one of my mottos and definitely how I've gotten through the last ten years. Watching stand-up, listening to comedy podcasts, reading about comedians, and studying comedy from afar has turned me into a comedy nerd.

> *The moment I can't laugh at something, I know I'm in trouble.*

We had one of those moments when Mom was sick, and I could tell her health was declining. Lying next to each other in bed, I would often watch something on my iPad before falling asleep. The lights were off, headphones in, and I couldn't help it, but I was laughing at an episode of *Arrested Development*. Mom told me to be quiet. She didn't want to know what I was watching, didn't ask about the story line, or care. It broke my heart because I knew if she couldn't laugh with me, we were in trouble.

When things were really bad, I hate to say it, but those moments of extreme pressure created diamonds in my life. I found my sacred gifts. They had always been present and cultivated, but maybe not named and fully claimed. When she died, I felt like I had no one in front of me anymore—to lead me, to protect me, to create space in the world for me to be in and belong. I felt cut loose, and not just from my mom, but from Spirit.

I joked with my therapist that Spirit and I were not on speaking terms at that time. Spirit was sleeping on the couch, and I was very much giving "talk to the hand" vibes. I couldn't believe this was happening. After years of fighting cancer and dealing with the ups and downs of treatment and recovery—three times—*my* person was actually gone.

After that, I shut the door on Spirit for a long time. It hurt too much to touch it. All those gifts and openings and sacred awareness were put on pause. It felt too hard—like a combo of touching a bruise and a hot stove at the same time, singed into my skin. I'd try praying again from time to time to see if it would still hurt. It did, over and over again. So I just stopped.

I stopped praying.
I stopped writing.
I stopped being willing to listen.

Touching the Earth or acknowledging her power was too hard.

Something and someone irreplaceable had left. That's how it felt—like she left instead of died. There was so much we were supposed to do together—lead workshops, write a book, travel to sacred places. The night of her memorial service, I pulled a tarot card alone in my room. It stopped me in my tracks and took my breath away: the shaman's death card. I placed it on my bed, closed the book that described each card, and didn't tell anyone. I couldn't face it. So I didn't. I walked away to join my family and close friends in the other room who were staying the night and did the best I could to wrap my head around this truth.

She hadn't "walked out of my life." It wasn't a choice. It was death. It was permanent. It was incomprehensible. For years, it felt like she was going to walk through the front door, having just gone away for a while, like I could hear her keys jingle in the driveway. But sometimes, especially with a long drawn-out illness, it takes a while to readjust your life and understand the person you loved so much is truly gone. There will be no more appointments for treatment, no immediate caretaking, no sleepless nights waiting on test results and trials. All of a sudden, it's just over.

We always said, "We packed a lot into those twenty-five years," and I hold onto that with all my heart.

21

Stripped Down

Have you ever felt like you've got nothing left to give? Have nowhere else to turn to find the strength you need to keep going?

I have been pulled to my knees twice in my life—stripped down to the point of seemingly no return only to "find it" at rock bottom, "it" being grit, resilience, the wherewithal to keep going even when I thought I had nothing left—the dig deep moments that teach us who we are; those pivotal moments of no turning back.

That may sound dramatic. But the truth? Each time I crossed a threshold, I clearly couldn't go back to the way life was before. And maybe even more specifically, I wouldn't be returning to who I was.

It reminds me of when people refer to "the new normal" after divorce or throughout this pandemic, seeking a stable place after the storm. We can't return to who we were, so we must move forward, not forgetting the trauma, change, challenges, and new possibilities that come from major life changes, but integrating them into this new path.

The first time I felt the rift in my body and soul—the no going back point—I stood in my kitchen in my little blue house in the woods. I lived in a small cottage set behind another house in Atlanta. The sun was shining through the kitchen window, and I was all alone. Not the logistic kind of alone like living by myself, but the kind of alone where I felt left behind.

My partner at the time and I had moved into this house together, broken up shortly after, and she moved out. My cat and dog from childhood both died that same year. I had nowhere to be and nothing to do unless I created it. I lovingly call 2015 "the year everyone died and left."

Two years after Mom died, I was standing in my kitchen, sipping a warm cup of Earl Grey tea, feeling lost and alone like my skin had been ripped off when she passed. I walked around as a fully exposed nerve. Part of why I share this is to demonstrate that grief takes as long as it takes. There are many layers to work through, and while everyone experiences it differently, there are things I wish I'd known earlier in my journey.

Flashback to 2012, I lived alone for the first time in my life. I moved home after college thinking I would stay for a year before taking off and traveling again. Then Mom got sick, and I chose to stay.

The trajectory of my life changed completely when she got cancer the third time. I took care of her in the house where I grew up. Right after she died, I inherited some money from a life insurance policy we didn't know she had, which allowed me to stay in the house a few more months until I decided what to do with it.

After counsel from close family friends, I chose to sell the house. It was just too hard to keep living there surrounded by all of her things—by our things—like the special knobs on the stove and the books in the entryway to her room. The plant she received when I was born and had kept alive for twenty-five years had started to wilt because I am not a plant person. That was her interest.

In several ways, I am quite the opposite of Mom. Every year for Mother's Day, she made us garden. I didn't like getting dirty, let alone spending hours doing manual labor. I just didn't get it. But she loved it. She loved cultivating and nurturing them. I preferred to watch trashy reality TV and leave the plants to take care of themselves. I lovingly tell people, "I grow people, not plants."

When I inherited the house, I felt cared for but with a heightened level of responsibility I didn't actually want. I wasn't ready to be a homeowner, and like I said, I went from living with the person I was closest to in the world to the absence of her. It was both strange and holy to stay in that space.

Truthfully, I wasn't really present for that experience. There was so much to do, tending to the logistics of death: dealing with medical debt, property taxes, her clothes and sacred objects. I was surrounded by *our* life together that no longer existed.

It's surreal to come home to the scene of a life ended, interrupted, and incomprehensibly quiet.

Originally, we all wanted Mom to be able to die at home. At one point, home care helped, but as her condition worsened, she became more and more dependent. And we needed more help than I could handle on my own. Toward the end of her life, we went to the ER for some unexplained stomach pain, which ultimately led to a week-long hospital stay and then transferring to a hospice facility, where she died.

The doctors gave her six months, but Mom died in three weeks. Time became irrelevant and all we did was eat, sleep, and wake up to face the horrors of the present moment.

When we were in hospice, it was a beautiful, almost cinematic time, as though her room was filled with water, and we were all just swimming in this weird in-between. The outside world didn't exist. Time moved both too slowly and too quickly.

We called Mom's students to say their goodbyes. One precious moment was when her students came for a final visit. I honestly don't know how we got so lucky, but this hospice facility didn't flinch with all the incredibly unconventional stuff we did there. From her room, we opened the French doors into the courtyard, which contained a small fountain and space to walk amongst some trees.

Standing in the courtyard, the smell of sage wafted through the air as her students smudged and cleared each other's energy. They were grounding and getting ready to talk to Mom and Great Spirit. Some of the women had worked with Mom as a client and then as a student for over ten years.

For many of them, Mom represented the good mother archetype—holding space for them, loving them unconditionally as they did deep personal work and stepped more into themselves. She'd seen many of them through divorce, moves, partner losses, new relationships, businesses, marriages, and having kids.

They stood in a circle with rattles and drums, singing songs into the winter wind. I sat by Mom's bedside and narrated to her, "Can you hear them, Mom? They're singing 'Earth My Body.' I think Cynthia is drumming, and Marie is singing harmony." It brings tears to my eyes now, the reality of inviting "the women folk," as Mom called them, to say goodbye. At that point, Mom was mostly not in her body but just hanging around in her energy field, listening.

I can't express my gratitude enough for that moment. It was truly beautiful to be surrounded by her students. It was a gift to see the living legacy Mom created and witness my own community stand around us—willing to come at the most vulnerable moments before death; to say goodbye and keep showing up.

I felt the waters rise in that room, and Spirit buoyed us. I could feel the energy of the people who weren't there in person and the waves of support. Being in that space couldn't have been more perfect. It was also brutal sleeping on the floor, waiting for Mom to leave her body. But ultimately, it was a true gift to have her pass at the facility instead of at home.

I never would've known that had I not experienced it.

Once we let go of the expectation of her dying at home, especially when I got back to the house after she passed, I was so grateful she didn't pass in the house. Allowing our human ego to guide us would have added an additional layer of difficulty to the process. Spirit's intervention helped us avoid the consequences of our original desires.

At this point, I would call myself an expert in my own grief; I've put in my ten thousand hours and know this is a lifelong process for me, personally. I want to honor that everyone has a different experience, but I also want to share how I show up for other people now based on my own understanding of grief.

I am especially interested in supporting caregivers because, all too often, they're trying to keep the entire ship afloat while they are actively losing someone. I spend a good part of my life discussing grief and hearing friends' stories.

Often responding with, "Yes, that's completely normal. Hate everyone around you? Normal. Clinging to the people you love now more than ever? Normal. Developing a slightly (or more than) unhealthy relationship with substances? Unfortunately, normal. Totally dropping everything you were doing to hermit for a while? Normal. Want to spend every last dollar left to you immediately? Or go into hoarding mode with money and material possessions your person touched? All completely normal."

Want to talk about it all the time? Or never?

Feel alone?

Feel a new level of freedom?

Feel at peace?

Have lots of baggage you're not ready to face yet?

All of it—completely and utterly normal.

You're not alone in your grief, even when it feels that way. There are people who understand, are compassionate, and can say the right thing at the right time. And then there are tons of people who will say the wrong thing at the wrong time, even when they mean well. And of those people—the ones who keep showing up—are the gems, even when they don't say the right thing, even when they piss you off. If they keep showing up, let them.

It will get better—gradually. But not in a "forever and ever, amen" type of way. In more of a one day, one time, someone will say the okay-est thing you've ever heard. And even if you're not thrilled with their response, it was actually not terrible, and you didn't start screaming at them, so that's progress.

In general, we are not taught how to grieve, how to show up for people who are grieving, or how to carry our own grief well. We all have preconceived notions of grief—how long it "should" take, what the appropriate responses and actions to do are, and above all else, when someone will "move on" and be "back to normal."

Notice this is all in quotes. Because guess what? Now, eleven years later, I still miss my mom every single day. It is different now than in the first two years, of course. Some of the painful sting is gone, but sometimes it's not. It just feels less jarring on a day-to-day basis. I've looked back at some of my writing five years into my grieving process and saw notes of when I was crying every day or being hit by waves of grief unexpectedly, not understanding why it still hurt so badly at the five-year mark.

At this point, I would call myself a grief veteran and enthusiast! When someone close to me loses someone, they often reach out. It's a beautiful space to hold for people, and it can be a lot. I have talked very openly about my grief from the very beginning and did my best to get through it. But I also had two really good grief models by my side.

One was a student of Mom's. We'd been training in the Medicine Circle for a couple years together, and she lost her brother and her husband within the same year, one to cancer and the other to a hiking accident. She had been through both a sudden and a more expected loss. Neither was okay, and both left trauma and sadness in their wake.

Mom passed a couple years after this, and Laurie stepped into my life periodically during Mom's illness to walk me through things. I had never truly "adulted" before, and Laurie had some really practical guidance.

The first thing I needed help with was sleep.

This is in no way medical advice, just my personal experience and something I wish I'd been able to read when I was going through it.

When Mom was sick, I was prescribed Ativan to help me get through the caregiving process as she became more and more dependent during the night. I needed some semblance of sleep, and after she died, I continued as needed. I had already had a history of sleep issues, but after she died, it shifted to a new level. I wasn't able to fall asleep before one a.m. I had to exhaust myself like a toddler to go to bed—exercise, cry, write, watch TV, and read until I couldn't keep my eyes open any longer.

I stopped being able to sit still with my thoughts for a while because it was too much to cope with. In the silence, I could feel the absence and presence of Mom in a visceral and uncomfortable way. It was really hard. I knew after she died I would continue to connect with her, but I really needed it to happen on my terms.

I want to share what worked for me, as it would've been so helpful to hear advice and anecdotes from people who lost someone really close to them, especially if they were part of their care team and survived that hell.

When I talked to Laurie, I mentioned having a really hard time sleeping even with medication, and she simply said, "Have you thought of asking your friends if they would come stay with you for a night?" Never had that thought crossed my mind.

I was so sensitive to being perceived as needy and asking too much because I had literally been told by people I was asking too much. Her decline went on for many months, and we had a high level of community support.

Amazing things happen when you're in the worst part of your life. People can be compassionate lifesavers, or they can get it so wrong, over and over again.

Unfortunately, there was a grain of truth in being worried about being too needy. A colleague who was by my side during this whole process told me, "I understand that what you're going through is a lot. But you can't keep asking for help at work. It's too much for us. Everyone is stretched thin already. Would you be able to just complete your work on your own? That way you're not asking more from the team, but you're also not taking on extra work?"

I felt crushed because, to me, continuing to work at all was a seemingly impossible task. I got where she was coming from, since we were all overworked and underpaid in non-profit, but when you're in a time of crisis—or as Mom called it, "up to your eyeballs in alligators"—you can't see anything except what you're going through.

So even with the support of the people around me, I knew I was asking a lot, and one of the sad but true facts of grief is that everyone around you will go on living their lives. It's very strange. They will face their own stuff, including crises and daily challenges. And as much as someone cares about you, your issues will drift to the background and become secondary. Because when you're not smack in the center of it, humans just don't have the long-term capacity to care in that way. Someone else explained this to me when I lamented as people gradually stopped showing up for me in the way they had previously. I didn't understand because I'd never been through it.

There is a time limit. It's not specific, like two weeks or three months. It's just a gradual shift. People can be really there for you, and then, one by one, they start to disappear after your loss. In the year that follows, it matters a great deal to have friends and loved ones around. After the meal train stops and people stop inviting you over for tender time centered around you and your loss, the harsh reality of moving on to the next cycle of grieving materializes.

Living with it long term.

So, in that small window where I had people's extra attention and care, I asked a friend to not only come stay with me at night but also to help me ask for support. This led to them getting my closest people's contact information and setting up a Google calendar to "sign up for a night with Meg."

This was a godsend. Basically, I had five people who would rotate taking a night to come be with me. Sometimes that meant eating dinner together or staying over at my house. Sometimes they slept in the other room, since there was an empty bed. My closer pals sometimes had a sleepover old-school style, staying up late, talking, and falling asleep together. Over time, those nights shifted to a few hours check-in and then gradually sleeping alone.

Someone would drop off food or plan to talk on the phone that evening instead of stay over. And then it shifted a little more to someone being on call if I needed it. And then it tapered off after about three weeks. That time meant so much to me. It was like emergency care. I wasn't used to being alone, especially in that house. And I didn't know how to adapt so quickly.

Those friends gave me a small runway to ease into full-time aloneness in my home. Slowly, though, they stopped calling, checking in, or coming over so regularly. They moved on. It was painful, but someone told me that was normal. I just didn't feel ready for the drop-off.

I wanted to be babied and taken care of. I lost the *one* person who used to do that. Mom and I were close in every way a parent and adult child can be. I can't tell you how many nights we fell asleep holding hands the last year of her life. When she was no longer on this Earth with me physically, there was a huge hole left behind.

This was the first time I was completely stripped down and had to learn to get up each day and keep going. Survival was literally the only goal. Screw thriving or pursuing big aspirations. Did you eat today? Did you sleep at all? Were you in touch with someone you love if it felt right?

That's all. Don't go start a foundation in your person's honor two days after they die. Don't quit your job and move to another country with no support. Don't start a business with zero experience and expect it to make a profit in six months. Or *do*... Honestly, it's your life. There are plenty of things I wish I had done differently during that time. But the truth is, I wasn't present enough to make those kinds of decisions. Years later, a therapist of mine said the first year, you're basically in shock. So surviving is truly the focus.

I didn't know it when it was happening, but there were entire months when Mom was sick that I don't remember at all. I was there, but my brain didn't log it. I very scientifically named these "periods of blackout sadness."

In those moments, your only job is to breathe and keep going.

It's not to excel, achieve your way through it, turn your trauma into triumph, or make your misery make sense. It's to keep getting through what's right in front of you.

Literally. This exact day, hour, breath—one moment at a time. That's all. And believe it or not, that's more than enough.

22

Intuition in Action

Do you ever get insecure about making decisions? Or constantly second-guess yourself?

Most of us receive an instantaneous gut knowing but don't always act on it because the Western world teaches us logic carries more weight than intuition. So we intercept the knowing with thoughts. We need to think about it and then overthink some more.

My family talked openly about trusting your gut feelings and tuning into the signals of the body, even if they were strange or inconvenient. Ultimately, this led to trusting my intuition above all else.

Every breath is a new opportunity to trust yourself.

This takes practice, and if it feels uncomfortable, just remember, you might be new to this. But if you've been leaning into your intuition for years, let's take it to the next level.

I love thinking of intuition as an indisputable competitive advantage. No one else in the world can feel or know or access or see the world the exact same way you do. With this perspective, there's no way to lose, and the only way to win is to trust yourself and your inner knowing.

If I were to add anything to the larger conversation about intuition, I want it to be about including the body. "Including" isn't even the right word. It's more about using the body as a source and home for our intuitive knowing.

Many articles, books, and beliefs reference intuition being held in the sixth chakra. Some people refer to it as the first or third eye, depending on their beliefs. While I appreciate having a specific place in the body to point to for our intuition, I am deeply passionate about broadening the scope of using the whole body as a resource.

I believe we can receive messages through intuition in and around our body at any time if we are listening. It does take practice to open the line of communication. I think of it as a radio frequency. Imagine being on a road trip and having to keep adjusting the radio town by town because your usual stations get staticky.

The more we play with that dial, the closer we can get to tuning into a more pure frequency. It feels like such a win to hit a station you like in a new place that comes through absolutely clearly. It takes tweaking and experimenting, dialing in to a new number intentionally. Like, rather than 96.1, in this new town, it's actually 103.3, noticing that 103.2 or 103.5 carry static.

Now imagine this is your intuition. Some people give up and turn off the radio before finding a clear station. That's what the majority of the population does, honestly. It takes a delicate dial, patience, and practice to find the right spot, especially if you're moving through multiple situations at once. (We're talking about life now…)

Seeing family, starting a new job, supporting a romantic relationship, and taking care of various pets creates extra static to filter through. The more emotionally charged a situation is, the more fear or level of pressure you put on yourself to "get it right," all impact how tough it is to tune into a clear intuitive frequency. There tends to be a lot of noise—both inner and outer—that blocks us from hearing our intuition.

Before we go further, I want to share some of my strong beliefs about intuition.

★ Every single human is intuitive (some are more open than others), but everyone can tap into their intuition and *choose* to develop these gifts.
★ *All* humans have access to Spirit and the ability to hear our own higher wisdom. This is not reserved for priests, rabbis, clergy members, or sages of any wisdom tradition.
★ No authority figure, doctor, shaman, or healer knows what's best for you and your body more than you do. They can absolutely suggest treatments, but it's important to still check in with yourself before blindly proceeding. If it doesn't feel right, trust yourself and your own knowing.
★ You are doing a better job than you give yourself credit for. I'm sure of it!

When you learn to turn up the volume on your intuition, it can heighten your other senses and literally shift how you experience the world, like that scene in *The Wizard of Oz* when there is a cinematic change from the world being black and white to everything in vibrant colors.

I want to magnify the *experience* of intuition, not the *how* of it but rather paying attention to it as a *felt sense of Spirit*.

I call it that because truly being able to *feel* Spirit is what changed my life and set me on this path. But I'm also a skeptic. I won't believe something because someone tells me. I need to experience it for myself and draw my own conclusions.

I'm curious: What changes when you consider your entire body as an entry point to intuition?

From the tip of our big toe all the way up our spine to the hair follicles on the top of our head, we are constantly taking in information with every inch of our bodies. Reaching below the neck or the mind is crucial for tapping into our intuition and full power as a sacred being on this planet.

One defining moment for me as a kid in truly tapping into my intuition through my body was during a fire ceremony with my family. My moms would build a fire together. Dreaming Bear took over the logistic side and prepped the wood, set it up with newspaper and kindling, and said prayers to Mother Earth and Great Spirit for this opportunity to connect.

Mom started to rattle and sing, calling in the directions, and we all joined in one of the songs we learned in the Medicine Circles.

We sang in unison several times as Dreaming Bear lit the fire with matches, walking around the circle to make sure the flames sparked on all sides. Seeing her kneel down, pull her hair back out of her face, and breathe into the fire is an image that truly captures her essence: being of service to the Earth, wanting to create a warm hearth for the people she loves, and illuminating the special connection she has with the land where she lives.

Once the fire took hold, we would sing in rounds, overlapping sweetly, our untrained voices hitting and missing notes, and singing with our palms open or on our hearts as our Teachers taught us; calling in Spirit, calling in the energy we wanted to work with that day, and bringing ourselves fully into the present moment.

I love witnessing people approach the fire. Watching someone transform right in front of us is beautiful, vulnerable, and unpredictable. Some people cry, while others get quiet, pray out loud, or gently whisper their words. The energetic transformation is truly gorgeous.

Mom always told me, "You look 'sparkly' after ceremony," like mud and residue had been cleaned off the windshield of a car and gotten buffed up and shiny. When I'm at a sacred fire, I get out of my own way and feel like I see clearly. Feeling sparkly is one of my favorite things, and this is one of the best compliments to receive. It's also a big reason why I love glitter, often telling people, "I want my outsides to look like my insides!"

That glow, that radiance, isn't from just being in close contact with the heat of the flames. It comes from shifting from overburdened to empty; from alone to held; from lost to Re-membering I'm part of this sacred universe.

Being in ceremony with my family is one of the biggest gifts of my life. It's better than when we went to see the Eiffel Tower, or when I got to eat at a Top Chef restaurant, or even when I graduated college. I can feel the powerful love the three of us built around many shared sacred fires, weaving together our prayers, songs, and dreams in that space.

In those moments, my entire being feels lit up by purpose. My body holds not only my consciousness but the chance to connect to the thing that feels like the absolute best gift in the world: being intertwined with the Creator, translating deep into my energy and soul. We are not separate from *them*. (I use "they" or "she" pronouns for the Creator. But use whatever makes you comfortable.)

And if that is true… if my body is fully inhabited by the original Source's energy… then how can we be anything but sacred?

On our saddest, most depressed days? We are sacred.

On the days we are not our bright and shiny self? Still sacred.

When you piss someone off or lose your temper or make a mistake... Still a sacred being of creation.

And when we show up on top of the world? Just as sacred.

Let's move this out of theory and into practice.

Embodied Soul Practice:

We'll start with a deep breath and neutral spine. You can do this sitting or standing. Go ahead and wiggle around in your chair a bit and let your body naturally settle into a small sway. Don't stop the movement. Whatever wants to come is welcome.

You're invited to close your eyes if that's comfortable and take a few deeper breaths. Imagine your exhale cascading down your back, almost like an energetic vacuum sucking up the thoughts from your brain and pulling them down your arms and legs and into a safe container. Those thoughts can be accessed after this exercise. They're not gone forever.

Keep an open heart and explore letting your body lead. Remember the exercise in chapter 12 where we used the Discernment ESP to discover what feels like a *yes* and *no*?

One piece I want to emphasize is if you're worried about getting it "right" or "wrong," stay open to the idea that in this moment, however your body responds is correct.

This kinesthetic response is similar to muscle testing.

You may even wish to give a mantra a try, such as: "I trust my body." See how that settles in for you.

Or if that feels too far-fetched, use this question, "What if my body knows the truth?"

All you have to do is open to the *possibility* your body is wise and worth trusting, even if you don't fully believe it yet.

As you give this a shot, feel free to ask more than one question and notice if your body goes into more of the yes or no territory. It doesn't have to be 100 percent. As someone who deals with anxiety, I made a deal with my nervous system that if I lean 51 percent or more toward one direction, that's my answer. It may be incredibly subtle. It may not look like swinging to the edge of the spectrum, but even 1 percent over the halfway mark is enough.

Notice if it's a strong or subtle response in this moment.

Begin with a gentler topic. "Do I want to go outside?" Depending on where you live, this may be an easy answer—if it's sunny or snowing, inviting or inaccessible. But instead of *thinking* about your answer, feel how your body responds.

Next, let's move to something you're genuinely curious about or struggling with.

Imagine the topic sitting in front of you. Now ask your body, "Is this a *yes* or a *no*?"

You'll gain confidence the more you practice.

For now, let's take one more breath. Thank your body for showing up for you today, maybe placing a hand on your heart and giving gratitude internally.

You can use this technique whenever you need support discerning if you feel drawn *toward* or *away* from certain topics. I recommend beginning with less emotionally charged subjects, and the more practice you get, the easier it will feel to access your *yes* and *no* to guide your bigger decisions.

This is intuition in action.

Intuition is the fastest moving human technology we have access to. It's sort of like telepathy between you and Spirit.

Nothing can get in the way—except fear. Fear gets in the way a lot. It stirs things up and can make it feel impossible to even hear the message in the first place. This is totally natural.

Fear turns clear intuitive messaging into a staticky call that keeps dropping. Like when someone near a very tall mountain tries to call you and service keeps going in and out. You get one syllable of every other word and try to fill in the blanks. When we're afraid, that's how it can feel to seek our own intuitive answers.

That's why honing the connection between intuition and your body is one of the most worthwhile focuses. The truth is no amount of tools, tasks, or years of spiritual training will get you further than your intuition will.

The ability not only to hear your intuition clearly but also to *feel* it move through your body creates a sense of knowing and connection to something bigger than us. That can look different for everyone, but ultimately, when your body, mind, and spirit can all access a clear channel, we are aligned and show up as our best selves. We can be of service, follow our hearts, and speak our truth because we actually know what's going on inside.

When you learn to trust your inner sway—of moving toward or away from something (a job, relationship, or opportunity) —you know your own power. Here is where our gifts start to unfold.

23

Create What's Missing

Whenever I attended personal growth workshops, I noticed my hips hurt from sitting too much. I would stand to take mini stretch breaks to compensate. Presenters often shared great content, but it only targeted the intellectual level with no attention or interest in integrating our bodies. As a kinesthetic and experiential learner, something substantial was missing.

I would go to dance class, and we would get right into moving. I've taken class with the same group of people back in Atlanta for over ten years, and there are some folks I don't even know what they do for a living, or if they have kids, or the name of their partner. Because we move together. That was our sole purpose for gathering.

I felt love for these people, but I didn't know them in a traditional way. We rarely exchanged words but still felt connected. I knew how people moved. I could see emotions flash across their face or could tell when they were having a hard day. But I read this both energetically and muscularly—rather than based on anything they said.

The specific dance classes I took felt very personal. I started taking class with this group when I was seventeen, and every time I came home from college or over the summers and holidays, I stopped in to take class. Over the years, I'd been through so many life changes, and my teacher, Ms.

Leah, was amazing. I feel very lucky to have studied with her for over a decade. She is half dancer, half philosopher.

She trained us with a keen eye toward improving strength and conditioning. Sometimes combinations stirred up emotions for me, and I felt tears form as I swayed my arms and moved across the floor. There just wasn't space to process these emotions in class—we had to hit the beat on five-six-seven-eight. I remember hoping no one saw when I teared up or caught on when a frustrated expression flashed across my face. It rarely had anything to do with dance but had everything to do with my life. I loved giving meaning to the nuances and intricacies of her combinations.

I brought all of myself to class, for better or worse. If I was super anxious, I had a hard time being present. There was a sweet spot for me in learning where the class had to be complicated enough to keep my brain engaged, but not so over my head I felt bad about myself. One day after class, a friend and I were debriefing and started talking about *why* we took class.

"I take class to feel beautiful," I said. "I like moving across the floor best, turning, flowing through combinations, and feeling good at what I'm doing." I'd been in class since I was eleven, and pushing, striving, perfecting, trying to get the same movements right over and over again; I was over it. I'd put in the work, been so disciplined for so long, and now just wanted to enjoy the good part.

"Wow." My friend laughed. "We take class for completely different reasons! I want to get my butt kicked and be told what to do. I want to get better and better."

"I get it. I remember that part. Now I just want to breeze through it. It was so hard for so long." My friend started this class just a couple years before and was more of a beginner in this style specifically. He was learning a lot really quickly. It was neat to witness, but it was clear we had very different intentions for taking the class.

By now, you know we hold emotions in our bodies, and using technique class to emotionally work through things was rarely appropriate. There's simply not enough time or space. Between all of these spaces—dance class, spiritual workshops, and coaching courses—I noticed a Meg-shaped hole, and the lack of engagement and integration led me to create the work I do.

I looked at what was missing and started to create it.

I wanted something more than a class that included a workshop-style space to debrief. I'm an emotional mover in many senses, and one of the best things I learned in leadership training is that if you're feeling something, it's likely someone else is too. So instead of being unkind to myself and worrying about what others thought or calling myself too sensitive, it inspired me to create the space I truly needed, that I hoped others needed too.

When I started choreographing in college, I saw a trend of traumatized dancers wanting to dance again after taking a break. They loved to move but had a lot of baggage around it. Dance-trauma is certainly real, and it took me years to acknowledge and understand how to name and address it within myself, let alone support other people.

I took what I learned from years of technique class and having a really harsh dance director and felt inspired to do things a different way. I wanted to make a space for both feelings and movement… to tap into the body to heal and process. I didn't even say this consciously to my dancers. I just started doing it. I created a space for them to be held and shift their relationship with dance and how they talked to themselves internally.

I wanted to teach them to put emotions *into* movement and use the often unkind narrative in their heads and flip it. The body *can* be a safe place but often isn't for a number of reasons. For career-driven dancers, the body can be seen as not only an instrument but an adversary.

"Not enough turn out, too tall, the wrong shape feet, calves, so on and so on." We keep correcting, molding, and trying to cram ourselves into the "right look." This is when dance is seen as a form for bodies instead of people.

I remember hearing more times than I can count, "I need six bodies stage left," instead of six people.

This can be dehumanizing, and dancers are often emulating the teacher or striving for perfection instead of fully embracing their own flavor.

I don't subscribe to this mentality anymore. And I see how dangerous and detrimental it was to listen to this dominant way of thinking for so long. I was literally told, "Meg, this is not a solo. You are part of a group. Look like it." I remember almost crying and running to the bathroom to hide. I didn't know how to look like other people. It was hurtful to squish myself down. And in this case, unfortunately, I was trying to with every aspect of myself—my mind, body, and spirit. Of course, it wasn't spoken about like that at the time. It was more an unspoken demand to be malleable and conform.

"You may want to think about losing weight before the summer intensive in New York."

"Watch Anna do the combination. You see how she stretches out her toes on the one and flexes hard on the three? That's the correct way. All right, everyone, let's go again."

"Fix your face!" was a phrase regularly yelled at some dancers in rehearsal, as their body movements may be beautiful but their faces were either dead-eyed or glossed over. The numerous small tweaks, nudges, and prodding by our teachers made us better. But it also made us different than our natural expression.

I want to highlight this aspect of dance because I didn't realize it was actually traumatic. It was never mentioned. It was just expected as "part of dance culture." Unfortunately, the impact of this doesn't just stay in the studio. We don't lose the muscle memory of correcting ourselves in a mirror over and over or the mental gymnastics it takes to keep performing with a smile even when injured. The perfectionism drilled into us definitely spilled into the rest of our lives and has quite a long-term effect.

Of course, the other side of this is the absolute freedom and beauty dance can provide. It's one of the only times I truly stop thinking and just be within my skin. As an overthinker, those moments are heaven. It's what always draws me back in—that and being able to express myself without words.

It's a gift to have an alternative to verbalizing concepts and be so present. We're just souls in bodies moving together. It's magical to lean into the moment. Sometimes time slows down, and nothing exists outside that space. It can even feel sacred.

Dance is where I first learned to touch energy and sense it between people. In our company, we took modern technique classes, ballet, and choreography, and had a big focus on improvisation. Improv simply entails making things up in the moment. Sometimes there can be a prompt or an exercise, but often, we started by moving to the music to see what organically occurred.

We played with improv a lot. You *had* to listen energetically to the people around you so no one got hurt. We were sharing weight, pushing, pulling, leveraging our own body weight, lifting people in the air, and moving together in duets, trios, and sometimes the entire group—with up to twenty people. I learned to use my peripheral vision and feel when someone was approaching, even if I couldn't see them.

There are all kinds of pointers and exercises to learn how to improvise with someone new, but there's also an unnamable synergy that happens when you find a good partner. It's a connection to breath, buoyancy, and an astute awareness that allows things to unfold effortlessly. It can be intimate and beautiful or clumsy and painful when you're off.

Over the years, I've danced with people in a way that has connected me to them for life, like their body's imprint was left behind on mine at a cellular level.

Really good contact improv can be incredibly intimate. When there's synergy and electricity in the moment, true merging can occur. I've led groups through an intensive contact improvisation session, where I've heard those exact words from participants: "I feel like you know me better than my partner." It's a safe place to let go and explore in an embodied way. It's definitely one of my favorite forms of connection when done well and incredibly unpleasant when done poorly.

Dance holds so much metaphor. I reflect on how every single correction or compliment I've received usually correlates to a piece of my life beyond the studio.

Here are a few examples I've received from teachers and my interpretation of how they translate:

"Your head is forward" means you're trying to think your way through this.

"Drop down into your center" is pretty self-explanatory.

"You are so good at traveling across the floor" means you are not afraid to take up space.

The metaphors are not lost on me, and I usually take time to think through corrections after class to find where they apply in my life.

If you've ever sat in a spiritual workshop, or gone to a seminar or conference and wanted to move your body but didn't want to get up and disturb anyone... I feel your pain. *And* if you've been in a dance, movement, or fitness class but felt the lack of community and space to really connect and talk about your life... I also feel you.

This is why I started creating workshops with space for both. It takes so much energy to create what you want in life. Truthfully, it would be easier if someone else would just do it. But there's usually a reason it doesn't exist yet. There's some piece *you* in particular can contribute to the experience that hasn't yet been explored.

Remember, the world needs your version, your voice, and your vision.

Your specific flavor, perspective, or slight adjustment could really resonate with others. And even if it doesn't, sometimes we have to do things solely for our own healing. I wish some of the workshops I've created existed when I was younger so my Little Self didn't feel so alone and out there.

A powerful idea to revisit is: "If you're thinking it, so is someone else." What you desire is needed in the space.

One invitation is to make a list of what you wish existed or to judge—in the best way possible—by taking something you enjoy but don't totally align with and write a detailed list of everything you would do differently. This is a powerful space of claiming what you truly want.

What are you craving that doesn't exist yet?

Sometimes we just have to be bold enough to create it, from that little version of you that needed it growing up to that adult version of you who is ready to step into creating what you need.

There is a *you*-shaped hole in the world, and *you* are the only one who can fill it.

What is calling to you to create?

24

Re-member Who You Are

"This weekend, we'll be focusing on Re-membering who we are, looking for the pieces we've lost along the way, finding the ways we've split our soul in the past to self-protect, and what is needed to come back into wholeness," Mom announced during one of the workshops up at Dreaming Bear's. The Medicine Circle gathered on an open-air wooden platform.

The gentle breeze during the day felt so good, while at night, without a fire, it would be too cold to sit comfortably in the fall air. Every workshop had a theme, and this one focused on the concept of *Re-membering*.

After opening the circle with prayers, Mom sat in her luxurious camp chair—it had extra padding, cupholders, and a footrest. This makes me laugh because it so succinctly captures the way I think of Mom as what I call an "air-conditioned shaman," someone who would prefer a slightly less rustic experience but still wants access to the wisdom of the woods.

"I'll be leading a journey with the drum to call back and claim the pieces we've all left behind, both consciously and unconsciously," Mom continued.

"We will be using soul retrieval as a technique to clear the pieces of any unwanted energy before calling them back into our auric field. This can be a powerful process and take a while to integrate. Please take extra good care of yourselves the next few days. Listen to if your body needs to nap, lie by the river, or connect with the sun. Recharging physically will help with the energetic shifts." Wrapped in layers of red, Mom scanned the group's eyes for understanding.

"Any questions?" She sat back in her seat.

• • • • •

Years after the workshop, I'd found notes from that weekend where I'd underlined the concept of *Re-membering*. It definitely felt like one of the most important teachings I'd received. My body shivered with resonance. Anytime I have a strong energetic response, I pay attention.

When "Re-membering" was mentioned, the word "memory" stood out to me. I could feel in my muscles some deep memories surfacing. But I didn't yet have the tools to clear and reclaim them, almost like scaling a fish, cleaning off the outer layer, deboning it, and leaving a more digestible version in its place.

I can't recall if Mom shared this image or if I made it up. But when we talked about how pieces of our soul are disconnected, hidden from trauma, or discarded to survive, I get the image of a large medieval torture device where people laid down on a large flat stone surface and had their bodies stretched to death, breaking bones by literally pulling people apart. It's gruesome, and as a teenager, I quickly changed the image to something a little more palatable… like playing with paper dolls.

If the figure of the doll was too short, when pulled in opposite directions, parts of their two-dimensional bodies would rip off, literally stretching the doll too thin. The extra pieces of paper would float to the floor, appendages seemingly discarded. Whereas, in the opposite direction, if the paper doll was too long or large, they would be folded to fit on the device, aiming to hide the undesirable elements and tucking them away to conform to certain standards.

In order to mend this doll, the pieces had to be put back together with tape or glue, realigning the seams and trying to make it fit like it did originally. In this teaching of *Re-membering*, the discarded or folded pieces of the body represent trauma, wounding, or a rupture of the body or mind and Spirit.

Some common times a part of the soul can be severed is during abuse, childhood trauma, car accidents, massive loss, or long-term patterns of pain. To me, this feels larger than responding by dissociating, as it's done subconsciously as a protective mechanism. Shamanic soul retrieval includes a process of finding the pieces of self we've discarded, turning them over in our hearts with a lens of curiosity, clearing the wound energetically (often with a trained support professional), and reintegrating the recovered pieces into a new sense of wholeness.

These soul pieces need to be dealt with gently, with healing energy and a discerning eye. If I was doing a soul retrieval with a client, I would create a collaborative journey going back to the wounding or general pattern they are wanting to heal and then clean and clear the old stories and heavy energy surrounding this piece. Then, once the memory is properly cleared and worked with—sometimes implanting more positive beliefs and stories, other times just reaching a sense of neutrality is enough—I invite the newly clean piece back in.

This can feel like plugging a leaky hole in a bucket. When pieces of our souls, our memories, and life stories are cut off by trauma and deep wounding, there can be more than just a mental and emotional impact. The splitting can also create an energetic tear.

When someone loses a major part of themselves, there can be a sense of being a shell of who they once were. Sometimes we pick up on a sense of rupture but are unable to target exactly what happened. Other times, it can be like a nail in a tire, a slow leak that takes years to acknowledge the whole impact.

I had a traumatic memory resurface from several years ago. After dealing with the initial shock, I asked my guides what happened and why it was coming up now.

The response was one of protection. "We held it until you were ready to deal with it." Ultimately, this gave me time to process and genuinely heal, but it also felt like a lot to carry on my own. I found ways to reclaim those memories and parts of myself that went underground through therapy, shamanic journeying, and energy healing with practitioners I trust.

We cleared out some of those hard memories, stripped them of any *hucha* (the Quechua word for dense or heavy energy), and reintegrated the clean energy. This is not to wipe out the memory completely, but to recategorize the story associated with that memory. It is also to remind the body it has the capacity to hold that memory with a new sense of felt safety. Not imagined, intellectualized, or theoretical safety, but an actual embodied sensation of reintegration.

There is definitely a parallel experience between shamanic healing and some Western approaches to therapy, like trauma processing and EMDR (eye movement desensitization and reprocessing therapy). I am not a licensed therapist and do not diagnose my clients or take the place of medical or therapeutic support. I do, however, facilitate healing on an emotional and energetic level—helping clear the energy field by finding leaks, obstacles, and pieces that keep people stuck or in pain.

Re-membering, which can involve bringing the "members" (the limbs and discarded parts of the body or soul) and piecing them back together, is a transformational healing process. I'm purposely not going too deep into the actual technique of soul retrieval because there are entire books written on the subject. Also, there are variations on the process, depending on the spiritual lineage.

I want to revisit the image of the paper dolls. As a child, I dressed them up in other doll's outfits, and sometimes the clothes didn't fit properly. It was like a puzzle, but I didn't mind if the outfit didn't come with the doll. I wanted to try it anyway. Once, I tried to stretch a dress meant for a shorter doll to fit a taller one, and it broke.

Mom helped me tape it back together, but it didn't look the same. There was a line now, a crack or wound with a noticeable tape bandage holding it together.

Sometimes soul retrieval can feel like that, even though we're healing, we have to face the reality we won't be the same as before. We have to adapt and mend by finding a new normal—a way to encompass the rupture knowing it will always be there. This can translate to having a tear in your energy field that will forever hold a history of rupture, like the doll.

Instead of trying to cover it up like it never happened, we work *with* the new seam, creating something different.

It reminds me of the Japanese art of *"kintsugi* [...] the centuries-old Japanese art of fixing broken pottery. Rather than rejoin ceramic pieces with a camouflaged adhesive, the kintsugi technique employs a special tree sap lacquer dusted with powdered gold, silver, or platinum. Once completed, beautiful seams of gold glint in the conspicuous cracks of ceramic wares, giving a one-of-a-kind appearance to each 'repaired' piece (Richman-Abdou 2022).

"This unique method celebrates each artifact's unique history by emphasizing its fractures and breaks instead of hiding or disguising them. In fact, kintsugi often makes the repaired piece even more beautiful than the original, revitalizing it with a new look and giving it a second life" (Richman-Abdou 2022).

A second shot at life is so powerful. We can't go back to how things were, but ultimately, we are made more beautiful through the process of healing. Like pouring gold into the seams to mend the body, we include the ruptures and tears in our story, and only *through* that we will find a new sense of wholeness and integration.

Re-membering is not passive. It is an active process that takes effort, patience, love, and forgiveness of self and others. This is no easy task, nor is it something to be entered into without a strong foundation of support both internally and externally.

We all have a reason for living or a foundational theme we circle back to over and over again. For me, this is healing. I've chosen to be fully committed to a lifetime process of healing. It's not always easy, but it is always worth it. With that declaration, I want to share:

A prayer for your own Re-membering:

Spirit,
I want to leave this life whole.
To pick up the pieces of me I've left along the way.
To call light into the cracks and jagged edges,
From where I've split from myself.

May I always have access to
Trust,
My own knowing,
And divine timing.

May Spirit speak clearly and surround me with Love
When it is time to face the edges of my soul.
May my inner voice and support crew on Earth
Know me well enough to see the new me
Thoroughly and completely, seams and all.

May my heart feel fueled by fire.
May my lungs breathe in fresh air.
May my feet be planted firmly on the Earth.
And may I decide when I want to move against or with the current.

May the parts of me that split know they have a home here always
In my body
In my energy
In my soul.

May I take the pieces I rejected
And recollect them
With Love.

May I wash them clean

With salt and rainwater under the moon
To weave them back into remembrance
Calling all the pieces of
Me home.

Deep breath, my loves. Your healing is in motion.

25

Follow the Childhood Threads

When looking for our life purpose, the grandiose idea we are all meant to find the exact one thing we're put on this Earth to do creates pressure.

What if we looked at it from a new perspective?

If you'd like to find, uncover, and tap into your purpose, let's go back to childhood together.

What did you love doing as a kid? What captured your attention so much you lost track of time?

A great place to look is also at what you truly loved but kept to yourself. Often, there are threads from childhood that give us clues to get back to our truest selves and rediscover joy as adults.

With this idea, we want to encompass all parts of ourselves. How would you describe your personality before the age of five?

Were you shy? Very trusting? Loved to bang on musical instruments? Wanted to retreat to your own space to play make believe? Or really loved being around people or animals?

We also want to look at what didn't feel good. Did you throw tantrums often? Get overstimulated and overwhelmed easily? Did you shut down your feelings because you were told you were "too sensitive" or "too much?"

All of these are clues to both pathways to joy and hints at where you may have had some unmet needs. For example, an early love of finger painting could have sparked a career as an artist or wanting to explore interior design. Looking at this thread can also create sadness for people—if they chose not to pursue it.

If an early love of art goes unnurtured—or worse, criticized—there may be a part of you that feels unsafe expressing yourself artistically. It can even go underground, not being touched or looked at for years.

It's not uncommon for a child to recall, "Well, my parents don't like my art. I guess I picked the wrong activity. I'm not really that good at it anyway." This can easily lead to a kid letting go of something they once treasured. This act of self-abandonment can also snowball and ultimately lead to a loss of trust within yourself.

I want to slow this down because that moment, where someone gives up something they love because they're not "good" at it by society's standards, hurts the world as a whole. There's not a lot of time dedicated to pure experimentation and exploration. As a society, we tend to be skill driven and performance oriented.

This way of thinking leads to shutting down or stepping away from what we love, robbing the world of a little more light. It's not that every single person will grow up to be the next Banksy or Beyoncé, but if our innate desires were given space and protected no matter how skilled we were, we'd see more people with their hearts on fire.

We're in an age where people are pushed to turn their passion into a commodity. You like to play with clay? You use it as a stress reliever? Well, now we want you to turn it into a business. Sell clay sculptures, sell beads, sell, sell, sell.

There's a much shorter timeline in the digital age of turning ideas into capital.

> *The ramification of sacrificing your own desire from childhood can lead to not knowing how to trust your gut, let alone hear your inner voice.*

These early experiences lay the foundation for what lights us up *and* what shuts us down.

This is how we get a woman in her seventies pursuing painting for the first time after getting told in third grade she was no good. It seems, with age, we grow back into ourselves. While it takes courage to step forward and truly claim some of those original desires, the part most people lose access to is *knowing* what those desires are in the first place.

Many of us have forgotten who we were at our core and got lost in the doing of life instead of the being.

Seeds get planted early on, and we either choose to water them and see how they grow; or they may get nurtured by an outside source—a teacher, a family member, or parent; or we literally get told *not* to water or pursue those gifts. Then they can dry up, go underground, or get lost completely.

Often, though, the seeds are not gone forever. They're initially planted with a small spark, in fertile soil that can be uncovered and nurtured back to life. As an adult, we get to consciously choose what we cultivate and put our energy into.

To have this not be only "an exercise," I invite you to take some time and envision your Little Self in their joy.

And honestly, if you didn't have a particularly wonderful childhood, *make it up*! Choose again. How would you like to rewrite your childhood? Claiming that is a major key to carving your own path and moving forward.

Embodied Soul Practice:

So, grab some paper and dig into your own story with this simple reflective exercise.

1. What three words would you use to describe yourself between the ages of birth and five years old?
2. What were some of your favorite things to do as a kid?
3. Go into detail with one of them. If you can, describe the activity you enjoyed, how it made you feel, and what you learned about yourself. What was your favorite location to do this activity? Add as many sensory details as possible: Were there certain sounds, smells, colors, visuals, tastes in the environment that made it important to you? Let this scene come to life.
4. After your response to the last question, write this sentence (you can put it into your own words):

"I know this is a little out there… but what if I got paid to (childhood activity) in the next (time frame)."

Let's take a breath and check in with your body.

Now place one hand on your solar plexus—the soft spot at the base of your ribs, a few inches above your belly button. This is the place of personal will, determination, and action taking.

Read your responses aloud to yourself or with a friend if you're doing this exercise with someone.

Sit with it for a moment longer, exhaling completely three to five times, taking slow, full, deep breaths.

How do these words feel in your body?

What are you noticing? Any sensations or emotions coming up?

Maybe there's tension? Elation? Disappointment? Concern? A sense of calm? Perhaps immediately overthinking or wanting to fire back: "How in the world will I be able to make that happen… this is so ridiculous… no one will pay me for…"

If that voice is coming up, the good news is your Protector self is stepping in to try to take care of your Little Self to make sure you make "the right decision" and don't go out on a limb risking the impossible. But here's the thing: When that voice comes in super quickly after you're writing about or even entertaining the idea of childlike joy, that means you're on the right path.

You're getting closer to a value that really means something to you! It could even be life-changing if pursued, so of course there's *a part* of you that's scared and wants to shut it down.

I invite you to pause here.

You're not committing to anything at this moment or quitting your job to run away and start your own blueberry farm when you've never farmed a day in your life. We just want to take a second to honor the sweet memory of picking blueberries with your family when you were four and how much delight that brought you.

The reason I said to play in this space is because it is in fact all about *play*.

Let your inner child know they don't have to be in control or figure this out. The only piece they are responsible for is naming the spark, which they already completed beautifully.

You are doing such a good job! I mean that. It takes courage to get this far, and if you are a treat person then now is a good time to reward yourself!

While picking blueberries was a client of mine's favorite memory, I've used this exercise several times over the last ten years on myself—especially when I felt lost or purposeless, questioning my very existence and what I'm supposed to be doing on this Earth.

The pressure and concern about timing can feel insurmountable when we try to figure it out. But sometimes the answer can't be deduced through logic but rather by *feeling* your way through and focusing on one practical step at a time. Connecting to one of your childhood dreams can tell us a lot. Does it feel exciting, threatening, enlivening?

Listen to yourself, because my sense is you can pretty easily tell if this dream is in alignment with the initial spark or core desire. Let go of what it has to look like for now.

Allowing yourself to vision and spend time embracing your dream and calling it toward you is an important step. It also takes action to turn dreams into reality. On the other hand, for my high-achievers, taking action with no space or attention to the dream can often lead to burnout, fatigue, and misalignment. This is when people drop their hands in frustration years later and ask, "How in the world did I get here?"

In order to avoid that, I'd like to share with you a concrete example of this exercise in action.

Here are my responses to the previous questions:
- The three words I'd use to describe myself as a kid: imaginative, smart, bossy.
- I loved making up stories and games to play with my friends. But more than just the games, I liked creating rules, obstacles, and experiences.

One time at a friend's house, we were playing with Cabbage Patch dolls and racing against an invisible clock to get the dolls dressed for a big party.

My friend and I pretended to be sisters whose babies were not cooperating, which made it rather hard to change their diapers and get them ready. Again, with a vivid imagination, I created obstacles to make the game more interesting. Of course, this in no way translated to being an expert at getting in my own way for years to come, clearly…

We pretended there was a clock counting down, and we only had fifteen seconds to get them ready. Shrieking, laughing, and trying hard to go faster and faster, we flung baby shoes and doll clothes around the room, making a bigger mess each time we started the clock again.

We kept getting close to zero and needed more time. So I would start counting again at fifteen, because I don't think I could count much higher at that point. We made so much noise, my friend's parent came to check on us. I was crying laughing and had little tears running down my face.

This moment of delight has stayed with me. I lost all sense of time. It felt like we played for hours. We improvised, made up a story line, added a sense of urgency, and tried to solve the problem. I loved all of that!

In this scenario, I also really enjoyed spending time with someone I cared about and laughing uncontrollably. It felt good to strive for a common goal together. I liked having a buddy to collaborate with and had much more fun than playing on my own. I also liked going to my friend's house to play because her family didn't have as many rules. Since Mom worked from home, we had to be extra quiet if I had a friend over.

I paint this scene to capture a moment of great joy and the meaning I pull from it.

If we work with the **ESP** above, how this translates to here and now as an adult is:

I know this is a little out there… but "What if I got paid to make up games with silly problems to solve, to play with friends in the next six months?"

Then I sit with: *What could that look like?*

To ground this even more, what if… just for a moment… it were *already* true?

What if I currently got paid to make up games, play with toys, read a book, paint walls fun colors, twirl, or entertain people?

What would be different about my life?

If I was already getting paid to create stories or games with obstacles people had to collaboratively solve, I imagine being part of a playful think tank. I haven't heard of something like this existing yet, but if I continue the scenario: *What would be different about me? How would I show up in the world?* This takes us into a sense of being.

I would have more confidence, excitement, and fun energy as I got paid good money to play, use my imagination, tell stories, and set up boundaries to create an engaging experience for people I cared about.

Can you feel the idea getting more and more grounded in reality as we allow the "yes energy" to take over?

It's sounding really cool. What is one practical step toward making this happen?

Maybe I would invite someone I cared about on a playful scavenger hunt. I could make up the parameters, invite them over... and we could go out in nature and search for a random list of objects and then make up a story about them at the end.

See what happens if you just keep saying yes to the idea? Follow the energy and see where it leads you. This doesn't have to be your best idea ever. It's simply a practice in separating the judgment that usually shuts us down. You don't have to commit yet.

This is another option to find what you care about.

When I step back, I see several pieces I value:
- Collaboration
- Creating something original
- Experiential learning with a focus on playfulness

Do you see what's possible if you go back to an initial childhood spark? Don't worry about monetizing it or figuring it all out. This exercise can bring new ideas to the surface. Give them space to breathe and unfold.

I don't know about you, but I am often drawn to things that don't yet exist, which makes it very challenging to find examples or specific paths to follow. I knew early on I didn't want to go to school for accounting, to then take a direct path to become an accountant. It just didn't feel right. I wanted a space to play with other people who wanted to work outside the traditional nine-to-five. I know not everyone wants that, but making space to hear what our inner child longs to return to can bring miracles into our daily life.

That part of us is very smart. We knew a lot back then.

The invitation is here to let yourself honor that spark and follow one of your threads.

What would be different in your life if in the next six months you pursued this path, one small step at a time?

26

Facing the Unknown

My vision for the future continues to expand and evolve. I love the term "emerging edge" as a way of classifying what we're moving toward as a collective. The space feels electric and alive.

The *emergent* world involves improvisation, deep listening, healing, and showing up fully. It means being present with the unknown and all our messy humanness along with our divine wisdom. It means living in a world of *both/and* instead of *either/or*.

We don't have to choose between believing in Spirit *or* believing in the power of community. We can hold both and dance between the two, weaving them together. Each person's gifts, ideas, and soul have space to be excavated and come alive.

As a concrete example, I envision a magical school where children's intuitive gifts are nurtured and adults learn to re-parent and care for themselves in ways they needed growing up. This is a multigenerational space for healing, where each person's gifts and truth are valued and honored. We have as much to learn from one another as we do from Spirit's messages and intuition.

It all works together, where we create a new sense of belonging.

To ourselves.
To Spirit.
And to one another.

Coming back to those three concentric circles, overlapping and informing one another.

Ram Dass and Mirabai Bush coauthored a book titled *We're All Just Walking Each Other Home*. That title fully reflects my belief of what it means to be a healer.

At the beginning of this book, I thanked you for letting me walk beside you for a while. I'd like to rephrase that, because as much as I love the idea of walking beside each and every person reading this, what I *truly* want is for us to walk together; to create a small contingent of embodied healers who live on the emergent edge, listening with electric stillness to people's gifts, wounds, and stories.

In the expectant waiting, we hold space to tune into a divine source of wisdom for what's *wanting* to be created next for our world.

In order to even entertain the idea of working on the emergent edge, we have to be comfortable with the unknown.

• • • • •

Since sitting with the unknown can be one of the scariest places for people, I want to invite you into a new way to connect with fear. Instead of demonizing it, conquering it, or sweeping it under the rug with positive thoughts, let's listen closely, invite it in, and let the fear take up space for a moment so you can learn what it's here to teach you.

Essentially, I'm suggesting feeling your feelings and making space so they don't squeeze out in other toxic ways.

Let's start here:
How do you visualize the unknown?

Is it a vast abyss where you can't see anything? Do you immediately try to problem solve by giving possible outcomes just so you have a semblance of control of something to hold on to? Are you a catastrophizer who goes down a deep rabbit hole of worry? Or do you blissfully turn a blind eye and stay in the present moment, unwilling to look forward?

Most of us will choose whatever option feels safest for our nervous system.

We use all kinds of protective mechanisms, and rightfully so. Your brain literally gives you a dopamine hit for determining *an* answer. It doesn't have to be *the* answer. The act of simply deciding gives your brain a chance to rest and settle. We get rewarded for making a choice. That's often why people jump from one decision to the next, rarely sitting in the space in-between, waiting for the answer to emerge. It's highly uncomfortable to stay in the liminal space. But the power of *staying* is immeasurable.

Staying, breathing, tapping in, and waiting for an answer to emerge reminds me of the concept of living into the question itself. Most of us are never taught to do this—to stay in a space of openness and availability, to make room to let the answer come to us.

Instead of releasing and relaxing into the moment, we often turn to distraction, worrying, and overthinking. If you've ever waited for a medical test result or the outcome of a job interview, you are familiar with this particular pain of waiting.

I'd like to experiment with a tool to help us sit with the in-between.

This exercise is really useful when making a decision, waiting on results, or even in supporting others when they need a listening ear rather than advice or problem solving.

In general, this "contained fear" exercise can help you sit with difficult topics without feeling stuck, jumping to conclusions, or holding back.

Embodied Soul Practice: Contained Fear

Let's start by imagining a beautiful container. You get to design it however you want. Is it a snow globe? A box? A glass jar? The only requirement is that it has clear boundaries and can be enclosed (top, bottom, and sides).

Now imagine stepping into that container and starting to take up space.

I'm going to illustrate with my own imaginary container. I see myself walking into a black box theater, closing the door behind me, and sitting on a cozy living room set—complete with twinkly lights around and a comfortable couch.

Take a few intentional breaths to settle into your image—very Alice in Wonderland style, no restrictions. You can sit inside a beautiful glass jar. Whatever floats your boat.

Now invite your fear into the space with you. Notice how the energy changes.

What does it feel like now?

How much space does it take up?

Is there a specific color, image, temperature, smell? Give it as much detail as you can. This can change each time you do this exercise, so just let yourself notice what shows up today.

You are in charge here; you decide how close to you the fear gets. Ultimately, we're going to interview it, so decide if it sits on the couch beside you or across the room. Just know it can't get closer to you than you want it to. You have the power here.

As you give it direction of where to be, start to examine it, maybe with a magnifying glass or a flashlight. Taking notes like this is the most interesting thing you've ever seen. Or it may be totally boring to you—in which case, that is also information. As you examine it, look at the *data* of the fear very objectively. How big is it, what shape, color, or form is it taking?

Now, here's the most important part of this exercise: *You're not here to change it.*

You don't have to fix it, feel comfortable with it, make it dissipate, or change it in any way. This is simply about learning to *be with* it.

Breathe that in. You're not here to change your fear, make it bad, wrong, or different in any way. You're not here to solve anything.

Take a step back from the image of your fear and throw something into it. This is purely experimental. Maybe you toss a blanket over it, or you electrocute it, pour slime or glitter on it... This can be extremely ridiculous or serious, depending on what you want to explore in this moment.

Watch what happens. Track how the fear responds.
Notice how you respond in this vision.
Take a breath.

And to end for now, either write down or say out loud, "I see you, and you're allowed to exist here."

That's it. That's the end of the exercise.

Again, no fixing, getting rid of it, or trying to clear it out.

To end this scene, we'll close by leaving the space—walking out a door and closing it behind you, putting a lid on the jar, placing your container within a larger one, like a box or vault. We just want to make sure there's a clear ending or punctuation mark on this experience. We're growing our capacity just to *be with* our fear and see what happens.

Wherever you are, envision placing your hands on the lid or door and speak your gratitude for your fear showing up today and for your own courage to face it and contain it.

Let's pause.
How are you feeling now?
Was it easier or tougher than you expected?

Just notice how your relationship to fear feels in your body in this moment.

This is a great exercise to repeat when you want to find a new way to be with your own "growing edge," stepping into the unknown or in the in-between without getting all tangled up.

Thank you for trying this and stepping into an emergent space. I envision us as a community growing our capacity to *be with* ourselves with more peace and lightness. I feel the ripple effects.

May we do so with love, kindness to ourselves and others, and space to listen and integrate the wisdom that lives within and around us always.

27

Centering the Body

Welcome to the Center. Center—the space where it all comes together, the space where you stand in the middle and look back at all the work you've done, the space of integration, cohesion, healing, and personal evolution. In this place, you can zoom out and see an overview of all the lessons and blessings you've encountered so far, leaving you with pieces of wisdom to carry forward.

Including embodiment practices with standing in your center is crucial. Here, we're combating the "enlightenment on top of the mountain" idea. Where you've taken the journey up the mountain, had an "aha" moment only to have it leave you on the way back down. To avoid that, we will focus on integrating new learnings and stepping forward on your path.

The way up will not look like the way down. You're different now, and using your body to integrate all the new learning and experiences you've had will help make a lasting impact.

Have you heard the phrase "What got you here won't get you there"? That's also the title of Marshall Goldsmith's book. Such a simple concept, yet so true. To paraphrase, doing the same things that got us to our present circumstances won't get us to our next evolution. When I heard that concept, I felt comforted and nervous, knowing the way I currently worked would not move me forward in my career, relationships, or spiritual evolution.

I learned the power of integration when I first started doing Medicine Wheels. I would go out on the Earth and have these beautiful, empowering moments where I felt physically lighter, supported, and actively healing. It felt refreshing and exciting. I would go "up the mountain," sometimes physically, other times metaphorically, asking questions of the Universe and receiving powerful responses—but found I couldn't hold onto them at first.

The messages from Spirit felt fleeting, leaving almost as soon as they came. So I started to play with embodiment and writing practices to anchor the wisdom from one world to the other. I wanted a way to integrate messages from the other side so nothing was lost. This helped solidify my experience of having a foot in both worlds without leaning too far in one direction and losing footing in the other. This meant finding a space to hold both the sacred magic and demands of daily living.

Writing sounds like an easy solution—to simply jot down the messages you heard. But sometimes you won't have access to a notebook and pen. I had to get creative and find other ways to help the new messages settle in. It reminds me of leaning into your strengths once you know your learning style. For me, as a kinesthetic and experiential learner, I lean into ways to connect with the body.

This idea came to me while walking the labyrinth up at Dreaming Bear's property one day. I walked around the outside of the pathway, turning to each direction and calling in support. Following the same pattern as doing a Wheel, I loved this labyrinth, as it was constructed inside of four stone markers for the four directions. This is unusual and focuses on the synthesis of labyrinth work within a shamanic context.

My moms built a "doorway" to welcome people to the labyrinth. The sacred entry point was made of vines from the land itself. This place holds so much energy and magic.

After calling in each direction, I asked for support in making a decision about a romantic relationship. I knew it was time to end it but wasn't totally ready to face what that meant and needed some extra guidance to help me take action and move forward.

As I walked toward the center, I asked Great Spirit, "Will you ground the answers in my body?" Walking over fallen leaves, damp from rain the night before, I felt a light breeze against my hands. Draped in a comfy long sleeve shirt, I pushed up my sleeves and placed my hands on the crystal at the center.

This crystal cluster anchors the labyrinth. It is about a foot wide and has points shooting in every direction. My intention was to anchor in what I was learning. It often felt easy to let things move through me, but that sometimes meant the messages got lost after an initial epiphany, like playing a game of telephone between Spirit and I.

But as I moved through the four directions, I kept repeating small phrases to help me remember once I was back at the house with access to pen and paper.

Kneeling down next to the crystal, I wanted to recap what I'd learned so far. Instead of just thinking my way through, I instinctively put my right hand on the back of my right heel, keeping my left hand on the crystal as an anchor point. "Remind me of what the South said?"

The message flowed easily. "It's okay to stand on your own two feet. It's okay to let go. It will be hard, but it's the right thing to do at this point." I invited that wisdom to run through my hand into my heel to carry it with me.

Moving my left hand to my solar plexus, I adjusted my stance to place my right hand on the crystal and leaned in. "And the West?" I asked.

"You are worthy of love. No matter what. It will come. Don't worry. We will protect you," my guides said, reassuring me by lovingly rubbing my left hand in a small circle on my sternum.

Being nervous about taking steps beyond the labyrinth, I repeatedly told myself, "I'll be okay. I'll get through this."

Placing both hands back on the crystal, the North message came in loud and clear. "Place your forehead on the crystal. Feel the Earth underneath you and surrender to this moment. Breathe into your third eye." After feeling like my third eye was filled up, I gently shook my head as I raised my gaze and rolled back up to sit on my heels. Feeling a little altered by the energetic transference, I kept my hands on the crystal.

"Sacred Fire, powers of the East, what messages do I need to bring home with me?"

"Bring your whole self through. You are welcome here. The right partner will see the pieces of you that you try to hide. There will be no need with the right person because they will see the world with the eyes of Spirit, and you will feel like you already know each other." I placed a hand on my heart, bowing my head.

Ready to take this wisdom with me, I thanked the crystal and center of the labyrinth for reminding me of the wisdom I had access to and could always carry with me. Once more, I touched the four spots on my body—the back of my right heel, my solar plexus, my third eye in the middle of my forehead, and my heart—like inserting a Post-it note in each place to return to when I needed it.

I love talking with Spirit. I feel held and understood here. I trust the words I hear and want to support other people in connecting and healing in their own way.

For me, integrating the body in my spiritual work has been a game changer. Especially since our bodies are talking to us constantly. Why not use that to our advantage?

This experience in the labyrinth happened over fifteen years ago. Focusing on consciously integrating Spirit's guidance into certain places on my body came to me intuitively and felt right the more I did it. I remember the smell of the leaves, the odd sensation of being guided to place my hands in specific spots, and having a deep knowing I was an extension of Spirit in that moment; that my body was actually a resource to be tapped into. This helped me claim the medicine I carry as an embodied healer.

It was quite strange to know what to do without knowing why I was doing it or what it meant.

For me, Spirit lives in the body (in all of our bodies), and my body lives in connection with Spirit. It's an access point.

Making tangible connections helped me integrate the ethereal wisdom and whispers from the Universe. I don't think embodiment is the only way to do this. I just rarely see it presented as an option. There is so much power in this underutilized resource.

While I would love for everyone to experience this felt sense of Spirit, it's actually more important to me to have each person discover their own way.

Your way may look different than mine. But when you feel that sense of settling in, it's like hitting the perfect note on the piano. There is a resonance that flows through your veins. Notice when it happens. What does it feel like for you?

28

Raise Your Energetic Awareness

Here is a somatic practice to build awareness of your own energy, explore setting boundaries, and create the opportunity to connect and hear the messages of nature.

In short, this exercise will teach you how to talk to trees and build your energetic awareness.

This is a simple way to protect yourself and set up an energetic container around your body. Not in a scary way to protect from negative energies, although this may help. I'm sharing this exercise with the intention of people learning to claim their space and set a barrier between what they do or don't want in their energy fields.

I can't tell you how powerful and important this is. Because once you start practicing and doing this weekly or even daily, you'll develop a more heightened form of listening to the energies around you.

Have you ever seen someone storm into a meeting late, frazzled and knocking something over on their way in the door? "Sorry, so sorry." They wince as they take a seat. Even if they're whispering, it may feel like the loudest anyone has ever been. That tornado of energy stirred the room, and everyone can feel the disruption, while the person making an entrance may not even be aware. This could be a simple inconsiderate act, but it also could be interpreted as someone not having *energetic awareness* of their impact.

Another example: After a toddler throws a tantrum and has calmed down only to look up and be surprised by all the blocks and toys they left in their wake. They were so caught up in the moment, they had no sense of the literal trail of chaos they caused.

Or when you're at a concert and the same two people keep bumping into you repeatedly. You may straighten your spine and use your elbows to create a barrier, taking a wider stance to command the space and stop the intrusion.

All of these are examples of someone being energetically unaware, which can translate to feeling like there's no respect for boundaries and personal space. While we cannot control other people's actions or make them behave a certain way, we do have control over how we respond.

This next practice is one I've done since high school. I use this technique before entering meetings, workshops, grocery stores, hanging out with friends, or going on a date—especially if I'm feeling nervous or walking into a higher-stakes activity.

Embodied Soul Practice:

Super simple.
Deep breath—full belly inhale, full belly exhale.
If you want, place one hand on your heart for a few more breaths to feel your own rhythm.
Now imagine a small light glowing inside your chest. As your heart beats, the light responds, expanding and contracting. Take a moment to observe it.

What is the texture like? What about the temperature? Are there layers? Colors? A halo?

Allow the light to grow and expand, taking up space within your chest, reaching out into all your bones and blood vessels, veins and muscles. Imagine the light bursting through your skin and illuminating your whole entire body.

Stay here a moment and pause.

What feels different from before? What sensations are you aware of? Any tingling or warmth? Temperature change or images coming through? All you have to do is keep breathing.
As you notice what the light naturally does, it's time to make a choice.
How big do you want this luminous field to be? Shaped like an egg surrounding your body, you decide how thick it is: only a millimeter thick, staying close to your skin, or many inches out beyond your physical form?
You can play with this.
What does it feel like to make your energy field huge? Still maintaining the outside barrier, expand and contract it close to you, almost like you're blowing up a balloon. Once you explore how tight or wide you want your field to be, settle into the spot that feels right for now.
It's your choice.
Again, there's no right or wrong way to do this. It takes practice and listening, or it may come through super clearly for you on the first attempt. Just keep breathing and noticing.
With this bubble or energetic boundary, you are creating a layer of space between you and the rest of the world. Truthfully, it's always there. We're just exploring what it's like to make this a conscious practice.

Feel what it's like to expand and contract the boundary—like wearing a big puffer jacket versus a slip. You decide how you want to show up today.

No matter what size barrier you put up doesn't mean you won't interact with other people's energy. This is more about adding a layer of support to stand your ground and ask for what you need. You can even decide to let someone in super close. It's all about choice.

The way we show up in our energy field influences our energetic impact. Notice I did not say *controls* the impact on our interactions but *influences*.

This is a great exercise to explore before you walk into a room. You can choose how big you want your bubble to be and notice how people respond.

What level of energetic boundary are you putting out there?

Making this an active choice can change your life. Especially for sensitive people or folks who are building awareness of their energetic impact, this is a great practice to explore.

Let's take another full belly breath.

Now that you know how to create a luminous field around you, I want you to try this out…

One of the most powerful energetic beings on the planet is trees. They have enormous energy fields and are very patient teachers. So the invitation is for you to set aside some time to go out in nature—your front yard, a local park, a forest… doesn't matter—and play with expanding and contracting your energy field in a safer context.

Simple steps:
- Choose a tree.
- Before approaching, introduce yourself and ask permission. This can be out loud or silently. "Hey, I'm Meg. Would it be okay to get closer and explore sharing energy?"
- Notice what the tree says. If you get a "No," simply move on to a different tree. If you get a clear "Yes," first set up your own energetic boundary and then slowly approach the tree. *This is a conversation.*
- Notice how your energy responds to the tree's energy field. Does it make you want to create a larger barrier around yourself? Or a smaller, tighter one?
- Does it feel good to be closer or farther away from the tree?
- Do you want to reach out and touch some part of it? A leaf, a branch, the trunk, or a root?

All good answers! We're just exploring. The invitation is to breathe and notice what you feel in your body.

- Then, when you are complete, stand a few feet away from the tree, or wherever is most comfortable, and thank it for letting you share some energy today.
- Before you go, send energy from your heart toward the tree to give your gratitude. You may want to put your palms out in front of you to send it love.
- Then pause, listen, and be open to any messages the tree wants to share with you.
- To close, place your hands by your sides, palms down, and send your energy down through your hands into the Earth. The position is not as important as your intention. Focus on releasing any and all energy you've interacted with today, back to its original source.

When you're ready, give your hands or your body a small shake to finish the release.

Take a few steps away, place a hand on your heart, take a deep breath, and allow any extra light beyond your skin to slowly dissipate back into your heart space, knowing you can access the light within you always, even on your darkest days. It may seem small, but like a pilot light, you can rekindle and expand it.

You have full permission to experiment and rest in this space as long as you want. May you move forward with your day with a little embodied boost of love!

29

To Keep in Your Back Pocket

When you feel stuck, or you want or need some guidance, use this short reference piece to come back to periodically.

The main questions to work with are:

How does that (topic, feeling, thought, belief, experience) feel in your body?
What meaning do you make up about it?

Intuition lives within every single part of our being. Some people access it more through their mind and thoughts (the mental realm), through urges and sensations in the body (the physical realm), through how something makes them feel (the emotional realm), or through the vibe or energetic impact (the spiritual realm).

Hard and fast rules do not exist in this book, because I trust you to explore what's best for you. **You are the expert of your own experience.**

The best guidance I can offer is to go into the silence of self with a *quest*-ion. Most spiritual paths involve a deep longing and seeking, a quest of the internal and eternal realms.

We learn to hear in the silence: ourselves, the messages of our guides and ancestors, and the Earth herself.

Feel free to revisit this as a whole system reset, or pick one direction that calls to you and explore what's here for you today. You can play with this for two minutes or an hour.

First, ask for support from the beings who love you. Then dive in.

South:
- What feelings are coming up for you right now?
- How "in the flow" or "out of flow" do you feel?
- What type of water would help you move through this with ease? Powerful waves? Rain? A trickling creek?

The South is also the space of heartfelt emotion. Listen to the inklings and inner nudges that are trying to get your attention.

West:
- What are you experiencing in your body right now? Tension? Space? Grounded, flighty, hot or cold?
- What part of your body are you most aware of?
- Notice what the current feeling is without trying to change it. Just allow it. As you breathe into it, let it expand and tell you more. How is it evolving?

The West is the realm of the physical, the body, and the Earth. Is there a place in nature that is calling you? If you cannot go there physically, you can close your eyes and hold the image of the place. Notice what messages come through and write them down.

North:
- What thoughts do you have about this topic?
- What's your vision for this idea?
- What's the wildest possibility you could dream up?
- Notice: Where are your thoughts? Do you hear them as messages contained in your brain? Are they coming from your heart or a certain part of your body?

The North is where we play with beliefs, thoughts, and possibilities. What limiting beliefs are you holding on to that you know you're ready to release? Give it to the wind and see what wants to enter the space left behind.

East:
- What are you *sensing* about this topic?
- What's the energy here?
- What images come to mind—the pace, tempo, texture?
- How flowy or solid is it? Does it have a shape or a color?
- Does it remind you of being a certain age?

Metaphors live in the East, the space where we move between birth and death—of self, ego, and how we relate to others. What would your ancestors or wisest self say about this? What is wanting to emerge?

In the Center:
Standing in the center, imagine the energy of each direction coming up to meet you. It can be fun to do this with colors of light, envisioning red light coming from the South and then black light from the West, white from the North, and yellow from the East.

Notice how each of these impacts your energy and what happens when they come in contact with one another. This can be a lot of energy, so keep breathing and paying attention to your feet on the floor, reaching down into the earth for grounding support.

Here in the Center, you have access to the greatest teacher of all time—your inner wisdom.

Exhale, my love. Trust you're doing it right.

The Center is the place of *Integration*. Imagine standing in the center and turning to face each direction from the inside.

What do you see from this new perspective standing in the middle looking outward?

What does it feel like above and below you?

Now, envision the very center of who you are…
Notice where you place "the center" in your own body.

Is it below your navel, in your heart, somewhere along your spine, in your feet? No wrong answers.

Pay attention, though, as this spot can serve as a touchstone for integration; a place you can send extra light or physically place a hand on as a reminder.

When you're ready, step outside of the circle you've been standing inside of, either physically or in your mind. Give gratitude for all you've received and experienced.

If you want to, now is also a good time to connect with your higher self.

What do they look like?

Do they show up as a guide, ally, teacher, or healer? An older, wiser version of you? The possibilities are endless.

Notice who—or what part of you—is guiding you forward?

What wisdom do they want to share in this moment?

Take one more deep breath, fully in and fully out.

Focus on opening your heart, mind, and body to receive this divine guidance. You may wish to turn your palms up to signify readiness to receive. Just breathe and hang out here for a few moments and see what comes.

Then, as you feel ready, close your hands together, rub them against one another, and make a sweeping motion downward so your palms face the ground by your sides. You can close this simple ritual by saying a short phrase or word three times.

Some of my favorites are:

Blessings, blessings, blessings.

    Or

Thank you, thank you, thank you.

30

Closing Prayer

As we come to a close, we have the opportunity to take these words off the page and into the world.

It is a gift to stand in your center *and* stay open to the support all around you. Imagine 360 degrees of love beaming toward you, lifting you up, and holding space for your most authentic self to step forward.

With so much love, I would like to close with a prayer.

Aho Great Spirit,
May the collective be held,
Stepping fully into our magnetic joy this lifetime.
Shedding what has held us back,
Old stories, beliefs, and assumptions about our limitations,
Clearing the path for love, support, reclaiming personal power, and healing.

May any energy that isn't ours be siphoned out and returned to its original source.

May love come up through the roots beneath our feet and overflow like a fountain through the top of our heads.

May our brains be kind to our bodies.
May our thoughts be in line with our souls.

May our hearts be open and our boundaries clear and respected.
May our bodies be safe and listened to.
May we hold ourselves with love and
May this path open to the realm of all possibility.

May we stand in solidarity with ourselves and trust our decisions.
May we be both the explorer and witness of our own sacred journeys.

May we feel the Earth beneath us,
Meeting this very moment with love.

May the Sky above hold space for our infinite dreams.
May we flow with the current, reminding us of the ease of moving around obstacles, and continuing on the journey toward what we want this lifetime.

May the sacred fire of desire illuminate our paths forward with wisdom, ease, and a little spark of creation in everything we do.

May we work to become good ancestors,
Cycle breakers,
Earth keepers,
And Healers,

Acknowledging how far we've come and how far we have to go.

May our souls guide us forward.

And may we hold our humanity and divinity in sacred balance as we walk with a foot in both worlds.

Acknowledgments

Thank *you* for reading this. I am so grateful you joined me on this journey!

Thank you to my family for shaping my life with so much love.

Thank you, Dreaming Bear, for fiercely walking your truth and choosing to be my OM.

Thank you to all the friends who listened, met me in coffee shops to cowork, and inspired me to keep going. Reminding me: "Done is better than perfect."

To my editors, teachers, and book guides, thank you for your dedicated time and energy. The book is shorter and better for it! Gina, Regina, Eric, Haley, Tanja, and Jesse, thank you for your craft and patience.

Thank you to this magnificent group of people who believed in, trusted, and invested in this book coming to fruition. I truly couldn't have done it without you:

Alex F., Alexandria H., Alla, Amanda, Ana V., Ann B., Anne Simone, Annette, Arlia, Ary, Ashyle, Aunt Carol and Deborah, Averi, Becca B., Bevelyn, B.R.E., Breanne,

Brianna, Brynna, Cara, Carrie, Cassie, Cathy, Chantal, Chris, Clara, Debra S., Denise, Dez, Donna, Emily, Eric, Erin, Faith, Glenn, Gwen, Heather, Hez, Hussein, Jacqueline A., Jacquelyn H., James, Jennifer R., Jennifer T., Joan, Jolene, Julia, Julie, Karen P., Karen V., Katie Mae, Katie P., Katie R., Katie S., Kayla, Kelly, Kelsey, Kenza, Kerry, Lauren O., Lauren P., Lauren S., Leslie, Lillian, Linda, Linden, Lisa, Liz, Lizzie, Lyd, Lynn, MJ, Magens, Marie, Mary, Mary Jane, Maureen, Meghan, Michal, Michella, Michelle, Mihal, Moraya, Nan, Nicolette, Nyle, Pauline and Nancy, Penny, Rachel, Randy, Rita, Robin, Ryan K., Ryan R., SD, Sarah, Saron, Scott, Sheila, Sophie, Star, Susannah, Three, Tom, Tony, Tori, Uncle Billy, and Zoe.

And I want to thank myself for showing up over and over again to get this work out of my body and into the world.

Appendix

Author's Note
Burgess, Matthew. 2015. *Enormous Smallness: A Story of E.E. Cummings*. Brooklyn, NY: Enchanted Lion Books.

Chapter 2: Make Space for Magic
Dahl, Roald. 2017. *Billy and the Minpins*. New York: Puffin Books.

Chapter 3: For the Love of Each Other
Raypole, Crystal. 2020. "A Brief Intro to the World of Somatics." Accessed April 8, 2023. https://www.healthline.com/health/somatics.

Chapter 8: The Last Workshop
Brown, Brené. 2010. "The Power of Vulnerability." June 2010 Houston. TED video, 20:44, https://www.youtube.com/watch?v=iCvmsMzlF7o.

Chapter 10: Spiritual Surprises
Andrews, Ted. 2018. *Animal Speak*. Woodbury, MN: Llewellyn Publications.

Chapter 13: Anxiety and Surrender
O'Neill, Patt, ed. 2014. "Inca Shamanic Glossary—H." Inca Shamanic Glossary. Patt O'Neill, April 2014. http://www.incaglossary.org/h.html.

Chapter 19: Finding My Place in Two Worlds
"amphibian." *Vocabulary.com* s.v. "Greek etymology of amphibian, n." Accessed March 30, 2023. https://www.vocabulary.com/dictionary/amphibian.

Chapter 24: Re-member Who You Are
Richman-Abdou, Kelly. 2022. "Kintsugi: The Centuries-Old Art of Repairing Broken Pottery with Gold." My Modern Met. March 5, 2022. https://mymodernmet.com/kintsugi-kintsukuroi/.

Author Bio

Meg Gibbs is a Somatic Spiritual Guide, Certified Coach, and Author. She has worked with hundreds of entrepreneurs, LGBTQ+ leaders, and creatives over the last 10 years. She helps people get in touch with their intuition, body and Spirit. Meg has studied shamanism since she was young, which has led to a lifelong journey of spiritual exploration with various healers and teachers from the US and South America. When not contemplating the mysteries of the Universe, Meg loves dancing, having deep conversations over high quality ice cream, and spending time with her dog.

For more information, visit: www.meggibbs.com.

CPSIA information can be obtained
at www.ICGtesting.com
Printed in the USA
BVHW051619160723
667251BV00005B/19